A CHRISTIAN'S WORST WITNE$$
FROM BEING BROKE TO BEING BLESSED

WHAT OTHERS ARE SAYING

"A Christian's Worst Witness" is just what we need to empower us to prosper in life. All of the principles are bible based and the advice is firm, and in the long run we will not be strapped by takers that have no desire to be integral. This book is sure to be a blessing to you.
— **Elect Lady Anetta Parker,
speaker and author,** *God's Grace is Sufficient*

I highly recommend Shalonda McFarland's book "A Christian's Worst Witness" for its comprehensive information. As the writers of old, it is evident that Ms. McFarland was led by the Holy Spirit as she provides practical solutions for the Christian and/or non-believer. Its readers will gain knowledge and insight regarding the abundant life that Christ speaks of through financial healing particular in today's environment.
— **Deidra Y. McCarty,
author,** *Messages...and How They Have Failed Us* **and** *Women of Color: The Challenges of Life on a Christian Campus*

Truly a God inspired book about financial stewardship. I highly recommend it. Read it and be blessed!
— **Farris Blount Jr. M.D.**

Shalonda is a woman of integrity and great wisdom. This book is a must read for those who want the will of God in their finances.
— **Pastor J'von Woods,
Tabernacle of Meeting Worship Center**

Shalonda McFarland captured the thoughts of God, his plans for his people, and the results of truly being blessed. This book is so spirit filled with power-packed biblical insights, and divine revelation that will revolutionize your life. Her message not only highlights truth, but it provokes change. Not getting this book is not even an option, it's a must read and a prayer answered to the body of Christ that will transcend to generations to come. Get ready to be blessed, it's your time NOW!

—**Nathaniel J. Brown,
Psalmist and Prophet of God**

A Christian's Worst Witness is an awesome book. This book has really challenged me to look at how I manage my own money. I have been able to witness to others about the importance of saving. Shalonda McFarland makes managing your money easy.

—**Lady Tracy Welch**

An awesome easy-to-read book with life-changing principles. An absolute must read!

—**Minister Dana Wilkerson**

Many Christians strive to prosper spiritually while they accept struggling financially as a way of life. This book enlightens us through biblical principles to have the correct balance both spiritually and financially. There are those that know this to be true through scripture that lack the wisdom to execute this knowledge in their own daily lives. Thank you, Shalonda, for allowing God to use you through this book to help Christians improve our witness financially.

—**Evangelist Sharonda Sanders,
Psalmist, Writer, and Actress**

Reading this book was truly an eye opener for me. It has given me a better understanding of tithing and I have been in church all my life. I really had to ask myself, "Am I a tipper or a tither?" Thanks Shalonda, this book has really been a great help.

—**Minister Perry Davis**

A CHRISTIAN'S WORST WITNE$$
FROM BEING BROKE TO BEING BLESSED

Foreword by
Pastor Christopher Welch

Shalonda McFarland

Purpose Praise Publishing, Houston, Texas

A CHRISTIAN'S WORST WITNESS
From Being Broke To Being Blessed
by Shalonda McFarland

Purpose Praise Publishing
P.O. Box 62425
Houston, TX 77205 U.S.A.

Verses marked KJV are taken from the King James Version of the Bible, Public Domain. All other versions used by permission from Zondervan via Biblegateway.com.

Cover Design by Brandon Boutté at
Visual Connections, Houston, TX

Book Production: Marvin D. Cloud
mybestseller Publishing Company
marvin@marvindcloud

All rights reserved. No part of this book may be reproduced or transmitted in any form or by any means, electronic or mechanical, including photocopying, recording or by any information storage and retrieval system, without written permission from the author, except for the inclusion of brief quotations in a review.

This book is designed to provide information on spiritual financial concepts. It is sold with the understanding that the publisher and author are not engaged in rendering legal, accounting or other professional services. If legal or other expert assistance is required, the services of a competent professional should be sought. The purpose of this book is to educate and entertain. The author and Purpose Praise Publishing shall have neither liability nor responsibility to any person or entity with respect to any loss or damage caused, or alleged to have been caused, directly or indirectly, by the information contained in this book.

Copyright © 2012 by Shalonda McFarland

McFarland, Shalonda
A Christian's Worst Witness / Shalonda McFarland.

ISBN: 978-0-9885651-9-7

1. Finance, Personal. 2. Spirituality

Printed in the United Sates of America.

2012921385

Table of Contents

ABOUT THE AUTHOR ix
ACKNOWLEDGMENTS xi
FOREWORD xii

INTRODUCTION: 1

CHAPTER 1: Faith 11
    He can be Trusted

CHAPTER 2: Obedience 31
    Are You a Tipper or a Tither?

CHAPTER 3: Giving 49
    Me First, Then You

CHAPTER 4: Living Your Dreams 85
    Nightmare on Your Street

CHAPTER 5: Planning 113
    The Eye of the Bull

CHAPTER 6: Saving 139
    Make the Buffalo Holler

CHAPTER 7: Borrowing 157
    Robbing Peter to Pay Paul

APPENDIX: 185
    Media Resources on Money
    Suggested Reading
    Bibliography

About the Author

Shalonda McFarland is an author, speaker, and entrepreneur. She has dedicated her life to the glory of God specializing in youth ministries where she has been teaching, speaking, and volunteering for over twenty years. Shalonda has also served the Christian community through advising, and helped with organization, fundraisers, and events. She has served on special committees, executive  councils, and leadership boards throughout Corporate America and within the Church. Shalonda's vast life experience has equipped her to be a wiser steward.

She is the owner of PurseString.com, which is a company dedicated to the financial health of women and whose mission is to Put Power Back In Your Purse. Shalonda also has her publishing company, Purpose Praise Publishing, which publishes intellectual property. Her articles on Christian finance have been featured in various church mediums and Christian publications including magazines and journals.

She is a dynamic, heart-felt speaker, who delivers a biblically-based message diverse with everyday examples.

Shalonda and her husband Doug have five children, Doug Jr., Mariah, Jordan, Melanie, and Rakaya, and reside in Houston, Texas.

Acknowledgments

All glory goes to God who has made this book possible. He has given me the ability, skill, thoughts, determination, and everything I need in order for this book to become a reality. Without Him, I am nothing.

I thank the man I was made to love, my soul mate, my husband, Doug for supporting me in everything I do. For the many sacrifices he constantly makes to allow me to do what I do, I am truly grateful. To my children, Doug Jr., Mariah, Jordan, Melanie, and Rakaya for their understanding and patience for the many times I've said, "I'll be through in a few minutes."

To Pastor Christopher Douglas and Tracy Welch, Bishop Paul D. and Cassie Landrew, the late Pastor Donald Powell Sr. and Linda Powell, the late Pastor Bennett Cortez Sr. and Lady Ruthie Cortez, and Pastor and Sis. D.N. Benford.

To Jacquetta Brown Smith, Diana Lynn Severence, Deidra McCarty, Brianne Smith, and Beulah Neveu for your insight.

To Farris Blount Jr. M.D., Nathaniel J. Brown, Minister Perry Davis, Bishop Richard Holman, Marilyn Logan, Dr. Jewel M. London, Deidra McCarty, Loretta Norris, Elect Lady Anetta Parker, Evangelist Sharonda Sanders, Lady Tracy Welch, Minister Dana Wilkerson, and Pastor J'von Woods for your kind words.

To Michael C. Brown Jr., Yolanda Davis, Ramonique May, Shannon McGautha, Cedrialind Rideaux, Linda Ross (my beloved mother), and Byron Upton for proofing and proofreading.

Foreword

When we look hard into God's word, we always learn something new about Jesus. Thanks, Shalonda for pointing to God's word and sharing biblical perspectives with us through your many stories and experiences in your book.

In the more than ten years I've known Shalonda McFarland, she has a deep and persistent passion in pursuing prosperity and wealth through applying God's word to her finances.

This is the best book that details why Christians are broke that I have ever read. Shalonda challenges us in this book to look at the importance of Faith, Obedience, and Giving. And now I understand more clearly that Faith without works is dead.

Shalonda can always be counted on not only to tell the truth but to pursue the truth with passion as she does in this book. In her unique, challenging, and careful way Shalonda breaks through stale superstitions and worldly beliefs about finances and shares with us a well informed, down to earth biblical perspective.

Shalonda, I admire and appreciate you for this book.

Christopher Welch, Pastor
New Direction Christian Community Church

A feast is made for laughter, and wine maketh merry: but money answereth all things.
Ecclesiastes 10:19 KJV

Introduction

You may be asking yourself, why I would write this book. I wrote this book because as a Christian, I was tired of not experiencing God's promises regarding money. I wrote this book quite frankly, because I became frustrated, confused even, of the examples I saw around me of Christians who had no money. I even found myself in the same broke situation. Yes, I had money to pay my bills, but I had little savings, and I was definitely not prospering financially.

I was so frustrated and came just short of asking God, "Is your word real? I mean the part about finances. If it's real, then why isn't it working in my life or other Christians' lives? If your word is real then why are most of the people I see serving you suffering financially?" Don't get me wrong, there are many Christians prospering financially, but for the most part the examples I saw were only on television. I did not see many prosperous Christians where I was, in church, in my family, nor in my community. Yes, I have seen small stints of success but nothing long-term. I wanted to remain financially prosperous as a lifestyle not a life moment. I also hadn't really seen finances being taught at the average church. I've heard it preached, but not taught.

There are many books about money so why write another one? Yes, there certainly are numerous books about every aspect of money. I have read and learned a great deal from many of them, in fact I've learned at least one thing from each book I've read. But when I've seen people in financial situations that a book would have helped, they were either uninterested in reading, couldn't relate to the messenger, or didn't believe the message. The perception of finance writers is they've gotten their riches through inheritance or off the backs of others. Hopefully, you can already relate to me through shared frustrations and as you read each page in this book, I'm sure the Holy Scriptures will emphasize my words and the real-life situations will depict what you have also seen. I've written a book that I expect will make a difference in people's lives by being relevant, informative, and causes you to take immediate action.

I realize that there are some who will not read many books, but if you want to gain financial knowledge and help, I suggest you read as much as you can about money. Immerse yourself in learning the subject you want to master, that is if you want to master your money rather than have it master you. It's been said that when the student is ready, the teacher shall appear. You'd be surprised how many financial learning opportunities will appear when you decide to learn more. (You can check the appendix at the back of this book to see a list of recommended resources on money.) The Bible has over 2,350 scriptures that talk about money, that's more than the number of scriptures that talk about heaven, and salvation! Why is that? Salvation, accepting Christ as your Lord, determines where you will spend eternity which is the most important decision you will ever make. Money doesn't even compare to it. So again, why? Is it because finances can cover many different things? Is it because that's where most of the mistakes are made? Is it because you will always be making decisions with money yet only have to say yes to Christ one time? Once you accept Christ and are saved, you do not have to make another decision about salvation. It's done. Once saved, always saved.

My sheep listen to my voice; I know them, and they follow me. I give them eternal life, and they shall never perish; no one can snatch them out of my hand. John 10:27-28 NIV

There are more scriptures in the Bible that make this point about salvation clear but this book is about finances. Nothing is more important than salvation of course, but being good stewards of God's money should be high on the priority list of a believer. So if there are so many scriptures about money, why are we still broke? Funny you should ask. This book will reveal a myriad of reasons but first let's look at a few underlying issues we Christians have.

For one, some of us are just plain lazy about reading God's word. Ouch! I know that hurts because it hurts me to think that. How much time do we spend simply watching T.V. compared to reading His word? When I think about all the time I spend doing worldly things and how little I spend reading God's word in comparison, I have been lazy too. There are many scriptures in the Bible about money but we seldom read, let alone study any of them. Even *if* we read, we do not look at the context of the scripture we are reading, we just find a verse that will remind us of the fact that God wants us to prosper. It is true, He does, but we take a scripture to try and justify our actions of something we have done or have the desire to do. For instance, if you need to buy a car and you go look at one that costs twenty thousand dollars and you know you can't afford it, you may pull out a scripture to justify your purchase...

But my God shall supply all your need according to his riches in glory by Christ Jesus. Philippians 4:19 KJV

Yes, He will supply your needs, but a twenty thousand dollar car is not a need. A car is not a need, it is a modern convenience. So maybe you've justified a purchase with a scripture. If that's what you've done, just recognize it and start to do things differently.

Another reason why we do not read His manual is we believe the Bible is outdated with a lot of stories that have little or no relevance in our lives today. So when we read about something in the "Bible Times", we dismiss it. There is no basis for this thinking however, it's just how we rationalize not reading The Word. Instead, we should look at the principles taught and apply it to our life. Principles are timeless; they do not change and the Bible is filled with God's principles which enrich our lives.

Finally, we *do* know what the word says; we just refuse to apply it. We think our ways are more modern, faster, and easier, yet we deceive ourselves. Beyond reading, the excuse we use as to why we don't apply the Word is we feel that a particular precept that the Bible teaches just will not work in *this* situation. All these examples are a broad explanation of why we remain broke and continue to struggle financially.

What about money taught in church? How many times do you get instruction on money at your place of worship? When money is mentioned in most churches people assume it is because the tithes are getting low or the building fund needs a lift. Is this a fair assumption? Also, it seems like the only scriptures quoted during service is, *"Will a man rob God?"* and *"Bring ye all the tithes into the storehouse"* Malachi 3:8-10 KJV. One can not hang their hat on these scriptures alone and never apply the others.

Another time money is mentioned in church or by a T.V. evangelist is when the sermon is about prosperity or when the evangelist looks at you over the screen and tells you to send a sacrificial "seed" offering to show your faith and in thirty days, you will get a breakthrough. Ministers do need to teach about prosperity among everything else the Bible teaches but when the sermon is over and all the shouting stops, what do you do next? There is little to no application to the fact that God wants you to prosper. What steps does one take to build wealth or should you be content with just getting bills paid? What money mistakes can you avoid? You see many believers broke and we know and have read that God wants to pour out his financial blessings on us. You have heard the quote, "The cattle on a thousand hills belong to Him" based on Psalm 50:9-10 and "His eye is on the sparrow" based on Matthew 6:26. Yes, I enjoy these and all other scriptures, but I want more. Hear me out; God is able to do more. He wants to do more than just supply our needs. Needs are clothes, food, and water, etc. What about wants and desires? He can and will supply those also. Our God is a more than enough God. *Ephesians 3:20 KJV says, [He] is able to do exceeding abundantly above all that we ask or think, according to the power that worketh in us... NIV reads [He] is able to do immeasurably more than all we ask or imagine, according to his power that is at work within us...* So if you are only getting your needs met, what's missing? Application. We are not applying His power (His Word) in our lives.

A Little of My History

"What does she know about finances?", you might ask. Simply put, I have failed with money and I have learned how to win with money. By no means have I arrived. I just want to impart some hard lessons I've learned over the years and hope that you will benefit from them by avoiding similar mistakes. We've always heard that experience is the best teacher but actually learning from other people's mistakes can be better. If you know the reasons people have financial issues, you will be equipped not to go down that same road. I've made many financial mistakes and have witnessed others making those same or similar mistakes and I've seen the tragic long term results of those actions. Out of all the mistakes that I've seen, heard about, and done myself, I know a lot of things that will not work.

Growing up in the 80's, I saw the struggles many families went through and I knew I wanted to have more financial options as an adult. Although I had little spiritual training as it related to money, the vast majority of my training came from the educational system and secular books. Some of the books had great information, while others were detrimental as they contradicted the Word with the newest fad or what sounded good.

The spiritual training I did have came from my mother who taught me to always, no matter what, pay my tithes. Not only did she teach me, and lead by example, she also showed me in the Word. As a result, I have consistently paid my tithes during my career, even through a period of time when I was out of a job. I was laid off but still had credit card bills and a car note to pay. Because of my obedience, God made a way for me to make every payment while still paying my tithes from my unemployment check.

Believe me, I was disobedient in other areas. I knew better than to have credit card bills, but I'll tell you later how that happened. I did not understand why I didn't have the money I wanted to when I'd always paid my tithes. So I searched the scriptures and read passages that I'd read before but now with the intensity of needing an answer. Not only did I read every financial scripture I could find, I analyzed them with the myriad of financial books you'll find in any bookstore, so I could better explain the practical implications of the Word. You may not always agree or understand the Word even though it is explained. There are certain things that I still do not "understand" but we still must do what the Word says and avoid what the Word says not to do. There will be times when we must take a leap of faith and defy all our human reasoning and simply—trust.

And when you hold up various situations in the illumination of scripture, although you may not understand why something will or will not work you simply must trust the Creator. Just as we trust humans--the inventor who wrote the owner's manual, the manufacturer who built the vehicle, or the scientist who says that invisible object is called an atom, we should trust the One who created all. We also have to evaluate the Word. If the word says to do one thing that automatically means do not do the opposite of that particular thing. For instance, when the Bible says to love one another, this automatically means do not hate one another. So we must examine what the Bible says and what it implies. Again, there will be times when we must reject our human reasoning and walk by faith and just do it. We have to obey simply because He said to.

For my thoughts are not your thoughts, neither are your ways my ways, saith the LORD. Isaiah 55:8 KJV

I've included real stories in this book as tragic, embarrassing, and even unbelievable, to encourage you that you're not alone in your mistakes. Yes, I know that at some point in all of our lives we will make a mistake with money. You may buy a shirt for example and when you get home realize that you do not know why you bought that color but can't take it back because you bought it from a store closeout sale. I'm not talking about the frivolous mistakes we occasionally make but the major financial fiascos we continue to make that keep us broke and unable to move forward.

It's amazing that as I was hearing about other people's mistakes I had 20/20 vision and was astonished that they could make such a grave error in their decision-making. It is a wonder how one can see other's mistakes so well when looking in from the outside, but when personally in the situation, we can not, or refuse to see the best way. I want you to know that this book is written for Christians, hence the title.

Followers of Christ should live abundant financial lives and yet this is more often not the case. I want to change that. Now that I've said that, if you are not a Christian, I hope that you would continue to read this book for the purpose of this book is to direct you to the Holy Bible. That is where you can see for yourself the truths of God, beyond just the financial aspects that I uncover. I hope that once you recognize what the Word says about finances is true, you will read more and be drawn into all of God's word realizing that everything in the Bible is meant to help guide us in this journey called life. All these reasons and the fact that God put a burning desire inside of me to help others is why I wrote this book. I want this book to be a blessing and a reference, and hope it leads you to The Book—the Holy Bible.

—Shalonda McFarland

Will you fear the temporary or have faith in the timeless, eternal God?
— **Shalonda McFarland**

Chapter One
FAITH

He can be Trusted

But without faith it is impossible to please him: for he that cometh to God must believe that he is, and that he is a rewarder of them that diligently seek him.
Hebrews 11:6 KJV

Trust in the LORD with all thine heart; and lean not unto thine own understanding. In all thy ways acknowledge him, and he shall direct thy paths.
Proverbs 3:5-6 KJV

You cannot have faith in just anyone or anything. Faith must be in someone who can be trusted, and we must be careful where we put our trust. Today people put their faith and confidence in the created rather than the Creator, in *things* around them rather than *who* (The Holy Spirit) is inside of them. When it comes to finances, we as Christians look out instead of looking up. How? Horoscopes, superstitions, signs and wonders, palm readers, the job, you name it.

Horoscopes

As a teenager, I used to always read the horoscopes for fun. Some people however, read them for direction, they place their faith in them. If the horoscope (written by a human being, I might add) says not to pursue something this month, then they will do what the horoscope says and not take action. The Bible never groups chapters or gives you a "sign" according to what month you were born. It is not uncommon to hear someone ask, "What's your sign?" And most of us know the sign our birthday falls under, however the Bible never gives a promise or character trait based on your birth month. The promises in the Bible are for all those who accept Jesus Christ as their personal Savior. Trust His Word not the horoscopes.

A wicked and adulterous generation seeketh after a sign; and there shall no sign be given unto it, but the sign of the prophet Jonas. And he left them, and departed. Matthew 16:4 NIV

Then said Jesus unto him, Except ye see signs and wonders, ye will not believe. John 4:48 KJV

Superstitions and Chain Letters/Emails

In addition to horoscopes, the following superstitions may be comical but some people really do believe in these:

- If a black cat crosses the street in front of you, you will have bad luck.
- If you break a mirror, you have seven years of bad luck.
- If someone sweeps your foot with a broom, you'll die early. You have to spit on the broom for this not to happen.
- The number 13 is unlucky. (Friday the 13th)
- If your palm itches, you will get some money.
- Knocking on wood gives good luck. (Do they

still rub that log on Apollo?)
- See a penny pick it up and all the day you'll have good luck.
- Eating black-eyed peas and cabbage on New Year's Eve brings good luck and prosperity for the new year.
- Horseshoes, Wishbones, Rabbits' Feet, Fortune Cookies, Elephants, and on, and on they go…

O.K. So you've heard of some of these and maybe quoted or practiced them from time to time out of habit. And yes, some of these may be "harmless," I look forward to my fortune cookie after a Chinese meal and have even kept some over the years. I just want you to realize how seemingly innocent things can creep up into our lives and without realizing it, we will have put our confidence in the cookie instead of Christ and if all it takes is eating black-eyed peas and cabbage to have money, we'd all be rich.

The definition of superstition according to Webster is a belief or practice resulting from ignorance, fear of the unknown, trust in magic or chance, or a false conception of causation. As Christians, we have no need for these useless superstitions because we are not bound by the traditions and hang-ups of other people, and we should be careful not to be influenced by them.

Be ye not unequally yoked together with unbelievers: for what fellowship hath righteousness with unrighteousness? and what communion hath light with darkness? II Corinthians 6:14 KJV

We really do need to be careful of what we say. We can "give life" to lifeless objects and create a crutch that will cripple our faith. We should quote scripture in response to someone quoting this superstitious nonsense to us. I'm not saying hit them over the head with the Bible but if they can speak nonsense, you can speak Truth. Some of us actually fear breaking a mirror or crossing a black cat, and chain letters are even worse. I get them from time to time through email and text messages. Let me say that God is not going to bless you simply because you forward 10 people an email, no matter how "spiritual" you feel the email is. Furthermore, God will not curse you and you will not miss out on a blessing because you did not forward the email.

God doesn't need gimmicks to bless you. It is nonsense that one would get an answer to prayer if they simply forward an email to 10 people in the next 5 minutes or whatever ridiculous parameters are included. And the tag line about if you don't forward this you are ashamed of your faith is just stated to make you feel guilty, not to mention that for some employers it is against company policy to send such emails.

Christians should not be caught up in superstitions when we have a supernatural God. If ever you feel caught up in the guilt of not going along with the status quo, or feel yourself putting more emphasis on what you think is just a "coincidence," meditate on some scriptures and know that God is in total control.

But my God shall supply all your need according to his riches in glory by Christ Jesus. Philippians 4:19 KJV

When I consider thy heavens, the work of thy fingers, the moon and the stars, which thou hast ordained; What is man, that thou art mindful of him? and the son of man, that thou visitest him? For thou hast made him a little lower than

the angels, and hast crowned him with glory and honour.
Psalm 8:3-5 KJV

Palm Readers/Fortune Tellers

Fortune tellers can be found in any city, by phone, and even on the internet. Even Christians may be tempted to use these "services." Why would you allow someone to tell you about *you* when all you need to do is talk to the Father and read the Word for your direction and your future? Comedians make fun of this industry all the time saying things like, "Have you ever seen a palm reader or fortune teller with any money? They can tell you about your life but they office out of their trailer. If they can see the future, how come they couldn't see the police coming?" Even though society jokes about it, this is nothing to take lightly. You may have been tempted to call a psychic to see if they'd give you some good news about your financial situation, but when the Bible mentions a fortune teller the person is said to have a spirit, an evil one, otherwise Paul wouldn't have commanded it to come out of the girl. Acts 16:16-18 NIV reads *Once when we were going to the place of prayer, we were met by a slave girl who had a spirit by which she predicted the future. She earned a great deal of money for her owners by fortune-telling...She kept this up for many days. Finally Paul became so troubled that he turned around and said to the spirit, "In the name of Jesus Christ I command you to come out of her!" At that moment the spirit left her.*

You've got to be careful what spirits you allow to come in contact with or influence you. It is unwise to give someone open-door access to your life when they don't have God's spirit. All of these are what the Bible speaks of as signs and wonders. You are to put your confidence in God rather than these things.

Investments

There are so many ways to invest money and just as many ways to lose it. There are many different investment strategies one could utilize. You have real estate, stocks and bonds, gold, offshore investments, capital investments, mutual funds, securities, you name it. Just as there are different investment strategies, there are also various ways to obtain the resources to invest. Some say use OPM (other people's money), others say cash only. There is nothing wrong with using different tools and strategies to make your money grow, but do not put your faith in them. The stock market can go from bull to bear in seconds and you can find conflicting investment tips in the myriad of financial magazines. Some advisers say diversify, some don't. Some say buy mutual funds, others say single stocks. You say gold, I say silver, and on and on. Although man's advice can be debated and therefore untrustworthy, you can always have confidence in the Word of God.

The J-O-B

Where else should you not put your faith in? The Job. Some even put their faith in the companies that employ them but just because you are employed does not mean you should place your trust and confidence in your employer. People get laid off daily based on the decision of a senior executive. People get promotions and move to different cities, only to have the position eliminated in six months. Just because you work for a big, "secure" company does not exempt anyone from the possibility of losing a job. Trust in God and honor the abilities He has given you, for He has given all of us gifts and talents and the ability to learn new skills. Your job may be taken away from you but no one can take away your talents and abilities, which you can use in any situation.

The Economy

Our troubled economy has led many people, Christians and non-Christians alike, to ask the question, "What if...?" The uncertainty of not only our nation's system, but the world's is causing worry and panic for many, but fear is the opposite of faith and if we don't have faith in God, we can easily succumb to it. I've heard it said that fear, f-e-a-r, stands for false evidence appearing real. Fear stagnates you, makes you second guess yourself and reduces your tendency to take risks.

If one is not a Christian, then you do have a reason to fear because you are not covered by the promises God freely gives to those who accept Jesus Christ as their personal savior. It's not trusting just for trusts sake. Jesus Christ is not just another option or choice among many to base your faith on. He is the only way to God.

If you have any doubts about that I recommend you read or see the DVD called "The Case for Christ" by Lee Stroebel. For Christians, this should enhance your belief and for non-Christians, including atheists, watch it to see why Christians believe what we do. If you are not connected to the promises that God gives, not only can the economy cause you to fear, but war and anything else can easily shake you and cause you to worry. But when you put your trust in Him, you can be at peace regardless of what is going on around you.

> *A thousand shall fall at thy side, and ten thousand at thy right hand; but it shall not come nigh thee. Only with thine eyes shalt thou behold and see the reward of the wicked. Because thou hast made the LORD, which is my refuge, even the most High, thy habitation; There shall no evil befall thee, neither shall any plague come nigh thy dwelling. For he shall give his angels charge over thee, to keep thee in all thy ways.* Psalm 91:7-11 KJV

You

This may be the biggest problem some of us have. Society has continuously told us to trust ourselves so we put our confidence in our abilities and in what we acquire from our abilities, sometimes it's not even what we own but what we're paying on. We trust our health, our intellect, our education, our networking abilities and connections, our skills, our wit, our strategies and agendas, our background, our family tree, our credentials, everything but our God. We are created beings with frailties and imperfections, so even with our best efforts, if God has not allowed a door to be opened for you, it will not be opened. And when God opens a door for you, no one can shut it because what God has for you is for you. No matter what, you always have to depend on God for everything.

> *For I know that in me (that is, in my flesh,) dwelleth no good thing: for to will is present with me; but how to perform that which is good I find not.* Romans 7:18 KJV

We've explored things that we wrongly put our faith in when our faith should be in God. Now let's look at a few evidences or character traits that show that we do not have true faith in God. In analyzing these traits please read this Bible excerpt and see if you can uncover the instances of lack of faith in God.

The Parable of the Talents

In the Parable of the Talents found in Matthew 25 the shrewd business man took the one talent from the poorest man and left him with nothing and gave it to the richest man. I used to think this was unfair. Why would you take the only talent this man has and then turn around and give it to another man who doesn't need it, the man who has the most talents? This is the same question we ask today. Why do the rich get richer and the poor get poorer? Why would someone rather give to someone who is already well-off rather than give to someone who is struggling financially? The answer…because the well doers have already shown they are good stewards of what they have had.

Listen to the surprising things the Word has to say…

*Again, it will be like a man going on a journey, who called his servants and **entrusted his property** to them. To one he gave five talents of money, to another two talents, and to another one talent, each **according to his ability**. Then he went on his journey. The man who had received the five talents **went at once** and **put his money to work and gained** five more. So also, the one with the two talents gained two more. But the man who had received the one talent went off, dug a hole in the ground and hid his master's money.*

After a long time the master of those servants returned and settled accounts with them. The man who had received the five talents brought the other five. 'Master,' he said, 'you entrusted me with five talents. See, I have gained five more.' His master replied, 'Well done, good and faithful servant! You have been faithful with a few things; I will put you in charge of many things. Come and share your master's happiness!'

The man with the two talents also came. 'Master,' he said, 'you entrusted me with two talents; see, I have gained two more.

*His master replied, 'Well done, **good and faithful** servant! You have been **faithful with a few** things; I will put you in charge of many things. Come and share your master's happiness!'*

*Then the man who had received the one talent came. 'Master,' he said, 'I knew that you are a hard man, harvesting where you have not sown and gathering where you have not scattered seed. So **I was afraid** and went out and **hid your talent** in the ground. See, here is what belongs to you.'*

*His master replied, 'You **wicked, lazy** servant! So you knew that I harvest where I have not sown and gather where I have not scattered seed? Well then, you should have put my **money on deposit with the bankers**, so that when I returned I would have received it back with **interest**.*

*'Take the talent from him and give it to the one who has the ten talents. For everyone who has will be given more, and he will have an abundance. Whoever does not have, even what he has will be taken from him. And throw that **worthless servant** outside, into the darkness...*Matthew 25:14-30 NIV

Many lessons can be taken from this text. I want to talk about the ones that affect your finances. God has given every single one of us gifts and talents. It is our responsibility and privilege to utilize those talents, to make them grow, to increase them to the best of our ability or we risk losing them. We should strive to be like the two servants who doubled what their master gave them. Just like them, we are to put our talents to use. It may not always be easy to do this but we have the responsibility to be good stewards over what God has entrusted in us.

Some people however do not utilize their talents, they do not realize their full potential. There are a number of reasons why this is the case and I want to explore a few of them. Did you find the character traits that showed a lack of faith in one of the servants? They are fear, no confidence, excuse prone, and jealousy. Let me explain them.

Fear

This servant who had the one talent was afraid that he would lose the one talent that was given to him so he hid it instead of putting it to work. His fear froze him to the point where he would not act. He was given an opportunity but wasted it because he lacked confidence and he made excuses for his decision. How many times has fear caused you to be complacent, OK with the status quo, or frozen? Fear is the opposite of Faith and is not of God. Fear is a spirit but Faith in God eliminates fear. Stop fearing people, the economy, rumors, the unknown, anything and everything. Fear, worry, anxiety, none of these are from God.

For God hath not given us the spirit of fear; but of power, and of love, and of a sound mind. II Timothy 1:7 NIV

Jealousy

Some people have the mentality that there is this pie that all of us have access to and if one person gets a big piece that automatically makes my piece smaller, so the more you get the less I get and vice versa. This is not the case. There are unlimited resources in this world and you have unlimited potential. Even though there are billions of people in this world no one has your exact finger prints. That's almost too hard to believe but God is so incredibly awesome. Just when you think you've seen it all, God allows someone to invent something no one's even dreamed of, to break another world record, to cure another ailment, to sell another million records. God planted into all of us unique gifts and talents that we are to use. Just like the servants, I might not have the same talents you have or the same amount, but we should all use what we have.

The problem is that some people are too busy looking at the amount or type of talents someone else has that they lose focus of what God gave them. Just like the master in the parable, God gives according to our ability. He knows how much we can handle and what we will utilize. The passage doesn't say whether the master gave his servants their gifts at the same time but let's imagine that he did. If that was the case, can you imagine what the last servant thought as he sees his master give a generous 5 talents to his fellow servant, 2 to the other, and 1 measly talent to him? This seemingly disproportionate distribution could make one jealous.

Sometimes the same scenario happens with us. Jealousy is like running track while looking back at other people in the race, so you're hindering your own movement. Instead of looking at how much someone else has and comparing it to how little you have, take what you do have and multiply it. Think about famous entertainers; some have the gifts of singing, writing, dancing, and acting while others only have the gift of singing. There are many people who have been extremely successful with their one gift of singing than someone who has all four of the above mentioned gifts. Can God trust you with your gifts? Even if you have just one, can you be trusted to use that gift to the fullest or will you lose sight of it because you have turned your energy toward another person's gift? You may want to be an Oscar-winning actress but that may not be the gift you've been given. You may instead have the gift of leadership and become the CEO of a Fortune 500 company.

Whatever your gift is, use that gift. It is an insult to God when we don't appreciate the gifts and talents He has given us and are jealous of someone else's, because we're telling God he made a mistake and doesn't know what He's doing. When you have faith in God and the fact that he is not a respecter of persons, you can avoid being jealous of someone else and rejoice for them because you realize that because they have "it" you can have "it" too. He is a Father to us all. Believe that He will give the same to you. If you have faith in God, you will not be jealous.

*...It's God's own truth, nothing could be plainer: God plays no favorites! It makes no difference who you are or where you're from...*Acts 10:34 The Message

In Christ's family there can be no division into Jew and non-Jew, slave and free, male and female. Among us you are all equal. That is, we are all in a common relationship with Jesus Christ. Also, since you are Christ's family, then

you are Abraham's famous "descendant," heirs according to the covenant promises. Galatians 3:28-29 The Message

In Christ, you are heirs and joint heirs. If you don't walk in your inheritance, it's your fault alone. Just like a check is no good to you until it's cashed, so have you not benefitted from the gift if you do not use it.

When Faith is Not Enough

We've talked about where we should not put our faith. I've reiterated that you must put your faith in God and Him alone, but just placing your faith in God is not good enough. What?! We went through all of that just to find out that even that is not good enough?! Let me explain. While you are continually placing your faith in God, you must do something else...take action. I did not make this up. The Bible itself says that faith alone is useless.

But wilt thou know, O vain man, that faith without works is dead? James 2:26 KJV

That's right, your faith, if not accompanied by corresponding action is useless. The "downfall of faith" is that we carelessly overuse the "God will make a way" phrase as a substitute for planning, and action. I can have faith that I will get a job but if I don't combine that with action, I probably won't get it. God won't do what you are equipped to do. The same goes with getting a college scholarship. You search and apply for it and try your best in high school to put yourself in the best possible position for the scholarship; you are putting action behind your faith. You don't get straight F's in high school, then pray to God to make a way. That's testing God and He doesn't work that way. Some of us treat God like a vending machine, we send our prayers up like coins being pushed in a slot and then we push the buttons that correspond to the candy we want. Prayer alone is not enough. Pray like it depends on God and act like it depends on you. Just like the woman with the issue of blood pressed her way through the crowd and touched Jesus' garment (Luke 8:43-48), just like the four friends of the paralytic man tore off the roof (Mark 2:3-5), you must act.

Faith is an action word, just as love is also an action word. In order to practice faith you have to do something, by putting action behind your belief. That is an *act* of faith. Not only do you act but you *speak* words of faith, so you have to watch what comes from your mouth; not only your mouth, but other's as well. Don't let other people talk you out of your blessings. Say God's words.

You must do all *you* can physically, emotionally, intellectually, and spiritually do while you yet pray that He bless your endeavors but you also must continually read the Word to allow Him to speak to you so you know His will. Prayer is speaking to God, reading the Bible is God speaking to you. Some of us are having one-way conversations with God. We do all the talking as we pray but we never hear God's response because we don't take the time to read His Word. Many questions we ask God in prayer are already answered in His Word.

Be careful of the enemy. If it doesn't line up with God's Word, it's not an answer to prayer. Case in point, I wanted money that I didn't have, for an investment. Sure enough, a credit card application came with more than enough money available to meet my desires. Is that God's answer to prayer? No! Be careful distinguishing between a blessing and a curse. Many times, as soon as we get through praying for something, the devil will send a copy cat first and since that is the first thing we see, we assume that is the answer God has provided. We don't even evaluate if it lines up with God's word. The enemy transforms himself as an angel of light (2 Corinthians 11:14) so he can imitate a blessing real well and disguise a trap to make it seem like an answer from God.

Things to Remember

- Parable of The Talents
- Track Race (Jealousy)
- Un-cashed Check
- Faith without works is dead
- Copy-cat answer

More Faith Scriptures

As for God, his way is perfect; the word of the LORD is tried: he is a buckler to all them that trust in him. 2 Samuel 22:31 KJV

Though he slay me, yet will I trust in him. I will surely defend my ways to his face. Job 13:15 KJV

O taste and see that the LORD is good: blessed is the man that trusteth in him. Psalm 34:8 KJV

Knowing this, that the trying of your faith worketh patience. James 1:3 KJV

But let him ask in faith, nothing wavering. For he that wavereth is like a wave of the sea driven with the wind and tossed. James 1:6 KJV

So shall my word be that goeth forth out of my mouth: it shall not return unto me void, but it shall accomplish that which I please, and it shall prosper in the thing whereto I sent it. Isaiah 55:11 KJV

I have no need of a bull from your stall or of goats from your pens, for every animal of the forest is mine, and the cattle on a thousand hills. Psalm 50:9-10 KJV

[25]*"Therefore I tell you, do not worry about your life, what you will eat or drink; or about your body, what you will wear. Is not life more important than food, and the body more important than clothes?*
[26]*Look at the birds of the air; they do not sow or reap or store away in barns, and yet your heavenly Father feeds them. Are you not much more valuable than they?*
[27]*Who of you by worrying can add a single hour to his life?*
[28]*"And why do you worry about clothes? See how the lilies of the field grow. They do not labor or spin.*
[29]*Yet I tell you that not even Solomon in all his splendor was dressed like one of these.*
[30]*If that is how God clothes the grass of the field, which is here today and tomorrow is thrown into the fire, will he not much more clothe you, O you of little faith?*
[31]*So do not worry, saying, 'What shall we eat?' or 'What shall we drink?' or 'What shall we wear?'*
[32]*For the pagans run after all these things, and your heavenly Father knows that you need them.*
[33]*But seek first his kingdom and his righteousness, and all these things will be given to you as well.*

³⁴Therefore do not worry about tomorrow, for tomorrow will worry about itself. Each day has enough trouble of its own. **Matthew 6:25-34 NIV**

Don't say, "Lord, bless what I'm doing," say "Lord, I'll do what You are blessing."
—**Shalonda McFarland**

Chapter Two
Obedience

Are You a Tipper or a Tither?

Honor the Lord with your wealth. Give him the first share of all your crops. Then your storerooms will be so full they can't hold everything.
Proverbs 3:9 NIV

Does the Lord delight in burnt offerings and sacrifices as much as in obeying the voice of the Lord? To obey is better than sacrifice...
1 Samuel 15:22 NIV

Tithing is the act of giving back to the Lord the first ten percent of your increase. This means giving God 10% of every dollar you make. You give it to Him through the vessel He's mandated, the church. Some may say that your tithes can go to any church or charity you choose, but this is not the case; this tenth needs to go to the church you attend not to a charitable organization. Charitable giving is commendable but those gifts are separate to what you give to your local church. Some would further argue that it doesn't have to be a church that you regularly attend, that you can tithe at one church but attend a different church elsewhere. On the contrary, you should financially support the ministry that is feeding you. It's similar to paying school taxes in one district when your kids attend school in a different district altogether. You should want your funds to go where your kids go. You would be upset if your child's school was in lack— the school not able to afford needed textbooks, too high of a student-to-teacher ratio, or desirable school programs and activities having to stop because not enough money was allocated to your child's school, only to find out the reason, your tax dollars were not allocated to that school but an out-of-state one. What sense would that make? Or put another way, would you pay your sister's bills and not pay your own. Why would you not financially support the ministry whose resources you are benefiting from?

The tithe is used to help the Church fulfill the purpose of ministry and in order for the church to function effectively it needs money. In order for ministries within the church to meet the needs of the people in the community, parishioners must give to the ministry. Examples of ministries include evangelism and outreach, marriage, singles, and youth to name a few. Another purpose of the tithe is to provide for the pastor, or overseer of the congregation. There are some who feel that the pastor should work a regular job and take care of his own family and not rely on funds from the church members and although many pastors do this, that's just not how God designed it. Pastoring is a tremendous responsibility that affects every aspect of a pastor's life. The office of pastor is a full-time job and God holds him accountable for the well-being of the people in his care. Pastors deserve to be compensated by the ones he serves.

For the scripture saith, thou shalt not muzzle the ox that treadeth out the corn. And, The labourer is worthy of his reward. 1 Timothy 5:18 KJV

I realize that when it comes down to money, tithing is usually the only financial concept that is talked about in churches and among Christians yet many still neglect to pay them. God is first and foremost, and whatever you have, He alone gave it to you. He allowed you to have it. I know it might not make sense to give 10% of your income and live off 90%, but this is an act of obedience. Why would God trust you with abundance when you are not trustworthy on the 10% that He commanded you to give back to Him?

The History of the Tithe

In case you have never heard of tithing, one of the first instances where tithing is mentioned in the Bible is in Genesis where Abraham (Abram) gives a tithe to Melchizedek the priest.

Then Melchizedek king of Salem brought out bread and wine. He was priest of God Most High, and he blessed Abram, saying, "Blessed be Abram by God Most High, Creator of heaven and earth. And blessed be God Most High, who delivered your enemies into your hand." Then Abram gave him a tenth of everything. Genesis 14:18-20 NIV

Another instance is when Jacob, grandson of Abraham, vowed a tithe to the Lord after he had a dream and wrestled with the angel.
And this stone, which I have set for a pillar, shall be God's house: and of all that thou shalt give me I will surely give the tenth unto thee. Genesis 28:22 KJV

God requires his children to give back to him 10% of our income, our increase. Some people argue that they can't afford to tithe. Whoa! You can't afford *not to*. God doesn't ask us to tithe because he needs money. He created and owns everything in this world. He wants us to give for our own benefit. Tithing shows our trust and willingness to obey our Father and as a result we are blessed. Let's look at the tenth this way. If I give you $1 and tell you to spend it however you want but you just have to give me ten cents out of every one dollar that I give you, that's a pretty good deal. And that's all God is asking for, 10 cents out of every dollar he blesses us with. We give Him 10 and we keep 90. (We give the government more than that!) Let's face it. If you aren't able to manage ninety cents because you say it's not enough and I give you ten more cents, do you think that is going to make a significant difference? If you mismanage ninety cents, you will mismanage the extra ten cents as well. God says in Malachi 3:8-12 NIV (you knew this was coming):

> *Will a man rob God? Yet you rob me. But you ask, "How do we rob you?" "In tithes **and** offerings. You are under a curse—the whole nation of you—because you are robbing me. Bring the **whole tithe** into the storehouse, that there may be food in my house. Test me in this," says the Lord Almighty, "and see if I will not throw open the floodgates of heaven and poor out so much blessing that you will not have room enough for it. I will prevent pests from devouring your crops, and the vines in your fields will not cast their fruit," says the Lord Almighty. "Then all nations will call you blessed, for yours will be a delightful land," says the Lord Almighty.*

So how can God bless you when you are robbing Him at the same time? What does the passage mean by "bring the whole tithe"? What does it mean to rob

Him with offering? The whole tithe question is addressed in Leviticus 27:30, 32 when God told Moses that the Israelites must give a tithe of everything that came from the land and of their animals. In reference to the offering, this can be found in the 18th chapter of Numbers where it describes the various offerings the Israelites were to give: a heave, meat, sin, trespass, and wave offering. Can you imagine all those lines on the church envelope? Thank God we don't have to keep up with all these specifications today; all we have to do is give our tithes and offering out of a grateful heart.

Effects of Tithing

You may not understand tithing but you will feel the effects of it whether you realize it or not, whether you want to or not. As the Malachi verse states, you will see positive effects if you obey or the negative effects if you don't. Just as you and I cannot physically see wind or gravity, we know it exists and we know the effects of each, even if we can't explain it. Wind can be calm and refreshing as it breezes through a wind chime or a spin wheel, but also violent and forceful as it whips through a town in the grips of a tornado or hurricane. With gravity, young or old, everyone is forced to live by the laws of it whether we want to or not, whether we agree with the law or not. A baby or a toddler are innocent and do not know the laws of gravity, yet they are not immune to the effects of it. If they fall off of a bed or out of a window, the effects of gravity will be the same to them as it would be to an adult who is well versed in the law. So not knowing the law does not exempt one from the effects of it, positive or negative. Just as that is true for natural things, so it is with spiritual things. Just because you may not know the word of God, that does not exempt you from the positive and negative effects, or consequences of your actions regarding obedience to His word.

Blessings of Obedience

Not only are there spiritual, emotional, and physiological benefits of obedience, there are enormous financial benefits as well. In the natural, a child benefits financially from their earthly father in two ways: needs and desires. Needs are supplied simply because the child is the father's seed and desires are given because of the child's obedience. For example, parents provide needs for their children such as food, clothes, a bed, etc., and based on the behavior of the child, a parent will provide desires like TV's, videogames, a restaurant meal, trip to the movies, etc. These are benefits. So what are some benefits of obeying God?

Here are a few mentioned in Deuteronomy 28:1-14

- You are blessed everywhere you go
- Your womb will be blessed
- Your substance will be blessed
- Your enemies will be confused and will flee
- God will give you a land and bless you in it
- God will establish you
- People will recognize that you belong to God and will fear you
- The Lord will bless you with abundant prosperity
- You will lend to many and borrow from none
- He will make you the head and not the tail
- You will always be at the top, never at the bottom

If you are not experiencing these blessings in your life, examine your obedience, particularly in your finances.

Curses of Disobedience

With every blessing that comes with obedience there is also a curse that accompanies disobedience. Many people are under a financial curse due to disobedience. Verse 15 of the same chapter begins to expound on the many curses which include confusion, being unsuccessful in everything you do, sudden ruin, and others enjoying what your labor has produced. Do you ever feel like your pocket has a hole in it? Everything breaks; you're either spending unnecessary money for repairs, or paying more than you expect on bills, or you may have even said, "It's always something!" These are all indications that you are experiencing financial issues due to disobedience and God has allowed the devourer to have reign over your money. The good news is that you can always turn it around. You can begin again. You can repent, start to live the life of obedience, and begin to experience God's best. Remember that you always have a choice. You choose your own fate. If there is anyone I'd want to obey, it's definitely the Lord.

How To Tithe—Your Paycheck

So back to the 10%, the tithe. Regarding your paycheck, what should you tithe off of, the Net or the Gross? Ten percent of *all* your increase means you should tithe based on your Gross income, the larger number, not your net income. The Gross is the *whole* of the increase, as far as your paycheck is concerned.

This is the money you make before any deductions are taken out--before income taxes, FICA, child support, health insurance, etc. Also, do not confuse Total Gross with Federal Taxable Gross which is lower than the Total Gross due to deductions like reserve accounts and health insurance. Let's look at both the Total Gross and the Net. Your gross income is your salary, how much you actually get paid. If you make $52,000 a year, that's $1000 a week. The first number on your check will say $1000 (the Gross) and then you might have before-tax deductions, after-tax deductions, and taxes taken out of your check. All of these items reduce your take-home pay, (the Net). If you are tithing off of your NET income instead of your GROSS income, you are not giving the whole tithe, since your tithe is based on your yearly salary, not your take-home pay.

So what should you do if you have not been giving your whole tithe all these years? Should you go back and tally up all the tithes you neglected to pay over the years? No, just ask for forgiveness and move forward. Instead of trying to go back and figure out the difference in what you did give and what you should have given, just start today of giving the whole tithe. The Holy Spirit may place it on your heart to give way above and beyond your tithe, to make up for the times when you did not tithe. If He does, obey his voice.

The servant who knows what his master wants and ignores it, or insolently does whatever he pleases, will be thoroughly thrashed. But if he does a poor job through ignorance, he'll get off with a slap on the hand. Great gifts mean great responsibilities; greater gifts, greater responsibilities!
Luke 12:47-48 The Message

Obey God or Man

I have included this section in response to women who have said that they do not pay their tithes because it goes against their husbands' wishes. Yes, the Bible does say to obey your husband in everything. Yet, you must read other scriptures and take them in light of yet further scriptures to get the full of what God is saying.

Study to shew thyself approved unto God, a workman that needeth not to be ashamed, rightly dividing the word of truth. 2 Timothy 2:15 KJV

Why would The Bible say study if we can just take one verse and run with it. We must understand the principles that support the scriptures as well. If your spouse tells you to do something against the Word, you are to obey God not man. Yes, that may at times mean going against what your husband says. Before you write me a disgruntled letter let me explain.

If your husband tells you to kill someone would you do it? Oh, is that an easy one to say "no" to? O.K. Steal? Cheating on taxes is stealing isn't it? No jury will let you off and drop the charges with, "My husband told me to do it and I was just being obedient," as a defense. In fact that will probably get you a first-class ticket to a prison cell. Bringing the job's office supplies home is stealing isn't it? And not paying your tithes is stealing isn't it? What if your husband says don't go to work until 9am or don't go to church? Where do you draw the line as to what to obey and what not to? So if your husband says not to tithe why would you rather break God's law than man's or society's law? So don't use the excuse that my husband doesn't want me to pay my tithes. If you earn a paycheck, you need to make sure you tithe on the paycheck that *you* earned. We won't go against the law of the land or the law of the office so why are we willing to go against the law of the Lord? Which is more important? Who will bless you, God or man? The consequences will not only fall on your husband, but you as well.

Remember Ananias and Sapphira in the 5th chapter of Acts. Sapphira went along with her husband Ananias and lied about their offering. Peter said, "You have not lied to men but to God." He later asked the wife, "How could you agree to test the Spirit of the Lord? Look! The feet of the men are at the door, and they will carry you out also." (Acts 5:9-10 NIV) This husband and wife both died because of the lie they told about their offering.

> ...*We must obey God rather than men!* Acts 5:29 NIV

The Tithing Loophole

I encourage you to be obedient to God's word and begin tithing, giving the first fruits of *all* your increase. This includes not only the money from your paycheck, but things you might not consider like bonuses, or monetary gifts you receive for your birthday. This also includes, in my opinion, any tax refunds you may receive because this is still an increase. I know you've already paid tithes on your income and this may seem like a doubling of your tithes on this refunded portion but this is still money that God is blessing you with. He is still the one who allowed you to qualify for the refund. I know Uncle Sam's name is on the check (actually it's the US Treasury) but God uses all kinds of sources to bless His people. Besides, if you had a choice, wouldn't you rather have a double blessing?

Why walk the fine line of this is tithes and this is not? Isn't it strange how we try to walk the tightrope of tithing? We want to give just enough to keep us in the clear of God's wrath so those of us who *are* obedient are satisfied with doing the bare minimum. We should stop looking for tithing loopholes and look for opportunities to bless God.

When we pray to God we ask Him to heal us COMPLETELY, to give us PERFECT peace, to love us UNCONDITIONALLY, yet we want to give God our crumbs, our afterthought, our tip, our "if I have something left over" money. Get rid of the fine line and look for ways to bless God, not ways to keep every little penny that you feel you can push through the "tithing loophole." How much would you pay for your health? Your peace? Your joy? How much are these things worth? How much is a healthy marriage or child worth? These are intangible blessings, they can't be quantified. Giving is an act of obedience and worship and flows from a grateful heart. Show the Lord how much you love Him by giving a sacrificial seed and showering Him with a financial praise today.

Also, when you file your taxes, make sure you claim the deduction for all your charitable giving inside and outside the church. Although your donations are tax deductible some people feel like they're not really giving if they're going to get a tax deduction for it. If you feel guilty about your gifts being tax deductible or that your giving is less noble because you file it just give your entire refund back to the church or calculate the tax return that you would get with and without claiming the charitable donations and give that amount back. Claiming these deductions does not diminish the motives of your gift in any way. The government incents taxpayers to give by allowing deductions. There aren't many tax breaks that some qualify for so take what the government gives you.

The Triple Threat of Tithing

The Houston Rockets was my favorite basketball team ever since I knew anything about basketball. Of course my favorite seasons were 1994 and 1995, when they won back-to-back NBA championships. There were many great players on the roster but undoubtedly the three players that would give the competition the most problems were Hakeem Olajuwon, Kenny Smith, and Vernon Maxwell. They were the Rockets' triple threat.

Just like the three best players on the basketball team, tithing is a triple threat. It comes in three forms. In addition to money, which is our treasure, tithing (and giving in general) also includes our time, and our talent. Although we've been talking about treasure, let me talk about the other two T's for a minute. As far as time, do we give Him the first fruits or minutes of every day? I know this can be a challenge since you already may hit the snooze button twice before you get up, but strive to give God quality time. Make time to read and study His word, pray, and listen to Christian programs that will deposit good in your life. If you find yourself consistently not having time for this, set up a daily appointment with God on your smart phone, at a regular time without interruption. He wants and deserves the first fruits of everything.

And talent, do we realize that He blessed us with our talents? We are only stewards over the talents he gave us. So do we strive to perfect those talents? Do we use our talents for His glory? Do we offer our talents for the kingdom or do we expect to get paid for our talents? There's nothing wrong with getting paid for the use of your talent but can't you offer your talent for free sometime? God's not charging you a royalty or a lease fee for using the talents He's given you but sometimes you need to use them in the kingdom, by helping churches and believers.

From Tithing to Giving

Now that we've gone in depth about the tithe, let me now drop something on you. Tithing was a mandate in the Old Testament which put us under the Law. We now live under the New Testament covenant which puts us under Grace. What does this mean to you? It means that the tithe being ten percent is just a guideline. Not only should we give the tenth, we should be giving more. Paying your 10% is good, it is an act of obedience, and is what we are supposed to do but tithers need to go beyond tithing and start giving, which is an act of faith. We need to stretch our faith and give above and beyond the 10%, to 12, 15, 20%, however God leads you. Or what about the pledge that Warren Buffett and Bill and Melinda Gates have made and are encouraging other high earners to make--to give at least 50% of their fortune to charity. (Oh, I took you too far too fast. Smile.) Wow! What would our churches and communities look like if we Christians would give 50%? Now that's faith! Well, something similar occurred in 2 Corinthians 8:1-4 when the Macedonian church gave generously despite their poverty.

And now, brothers and sisters, we want you to know about the grace that God has given the Macedonian churches. In the midst of a very severe trial, their overflowing joy and their extreme poverty welled up in rich generosity. For I testify that they gave as much as they were able, and even beyond their ability. Entirely on their own, they urgently pleaded with us for the privilege of sharing in this service to the Lord's people. 2 Corinthians 8:1-4 NIV

You may be giving 11% this year and 14% the next. Just start somewhere and watch and see how God responds. You will experience favor like you've never known.

Isn't it amazing, that God does not make us do anything. He did not create us to be robots, that blindly follow every preprogrammed command. No, he doesn't make us do anything, not even love him. He gives us free will to make our own choices. In giving, we must trust Him. That's good news because He is trustworthy. He is not like man. We don't trust Uncle Sam and he does not trust us, that's why he takes taxes out of our check before we get a dime and sales tax is added directly to the ticket of virtually everything we buy. Gratuity is even added to your restaurant bill, yet God, who made us, trusts us enough to let *us* give back to Him a portion of what He already gave to us. He gives us a guideline of 10% and also says we should purpose in our hearts what we should give.

Remember this: Whoever sows sparingly will also reap sparingly, and whoever sows generously will also reap generously. Each man should give what he has decided in his heart to give, not reluctantly or under compulsion, for God loves a cheerful giver. 2 Corinthians 9:6-7 NIV

The tithe is an act of obedience, and anything above and beyond is our offering to God. If you won't bless God with money he has given you, he won't bless you to bless others. You are blessed to be a blessing. It is impossible to beat God's giving, so give generously from your heart. Are you a tipper or a tither? I hope you answer, "I am a Giver!"

Things to Remember

- Effects of Gravity
- Tithing tightrope
- Tithing loophole
- Tithing triple threat
- Gross vs Net
- From Tithing to Giving

More Obedience Scriptures

"Give to Caesar what is Caesar's, and to God what is God's." Matthew 22:21 NIV

So if you have not been trustworthy in handling worldly wealth, who will trust you with true riches? Luke 16:11 NIV

Delight yourself in the LORD and he will give you the desires of your heart. Psalm 37:4 NIV

As obedient children, do not conform to the evil desires you had when you lived in ignorance. 1 Peter 1:14 NIV

Do not be deceived: God cannot be mocked. A man reaps what he sows. Galatians 6:7 NIV

Woe unto you, scribes and Pharisees, hypocrites! for ye pay tithe of mint and anise and cummin, and have omitted the weightier matters of the law, judgment, mercy, and

faith: these ought ye to have done, and not to leave the other undone. Matthew 23:23 KJV

At the end of every three years, bring all the tithes of that year's produce and store it in your towns, so that the Levites (who have no allotment or inheritance of their own) and the aliens, the fatherless and the widows who live in your towns may come and eat and be satisfied, and so that the LORD your God may bless you in all the work of your hands. Deuteronomy 14:28-29 NIV

The LORD said to Moses, "Tell the Israelites to bring me an offering. You are to receive the offering for me from everyone whose heart prompts them to give. Exodus 25:1-2 NIV

They received from Moses all the offerings the Israelites had brought to carry out the work of constructing the sanctuary. And the people continued to bring freewill offerings morning after morning. So all the skilled workers who were doing all the work on the sanctuary left what they were doing and said to Moses, "The people are bringing more than enough for doing the work the LORD commanded to be done." Exodus 36:3-5 NIV

God won't pour a blessing into a clogged pipe.
—**Shalonda McFarland**

Chapter Three
Giving

Me First, Then You

One person gives freely, yet gains even more; another withholds unduly, but comes to poverty. A generous person will prosper; whoever refreshes others will be refreshed.
Proverbs 11:24-25 NIV

I have shewed you all things, how that so labouring ye ought to support the weak, and to remember the words of the Lord Jesus, how he said, It is more blessed to give than to receive.
Acts 20:35 KJV

Of course you can't have a book about money without a chapter on giving. I will touch on why we should give, hence the two scriptures above, but most people already know that. Most of us give because it is our nature to give. The very example of Christ was to give the ultimate gift, his life. So since we are Christians, we have the perfect example of giving, to God and others.

However, what I really want to discuss is why we should *not* give (the benefits of not giving), when we should not give (the circumstances under which we should not give), and who we should not give to. When you think of giving, keep this visual in your mind. During a plane flight there is one safety procedure that is one of the best ways to explain the principle of giving. Can you guess what it is? First, the stewardess says, "slide the medal end of the buckle...12 exits in this aircraft but keep in mind that the nearest exit may be behind you...life vest and if we experience a sudden decrease in cabin pressure, oxygen masks will drop from the ceiling. To start the flow of oxygen put the mask over your nose and mouth, tighten the elastic band around your head by pulling on either side"...then the stewardess gives us this profound detailed instruction "put *your* mask on first before assisting other customers" or "remember to first place the mask over your face, then secure the mask over the child's face."

Did you get that? Please let that sink in. The natural instinct of a mother is to protect the child first, so it makes sense to put the oxygen mask over your cute little child's face before you protect your own. But this would be wrong and under the right circumstances, deadly. To protect both you and your child, you must put the mask on *you* first, then your baby.

Wow. I know you see the application by now. In order to preserve both of your lives, you must fight the natural instinct of seeing to their needs before your own, and think about *you* first. In order for you both to live you must ensure your needs are met first before you can attend to your child's or anyone else's needs. This is the same way we should view money. I hope you'll allow those flight instructions to be a constant financial reminder. So in order to give, you must first have something to give. You can't give something that you do not have to someone else. You can not deny your own needs, nor your own family's needs, to take care of another person's needs, no matter who they are.

But if anyone does not provide for his own, and especially for those of his household, he has denied the faith and is worse than an unbeliever. 1 Timothy 5:8 NKJV

If you are married, you are one with your spouse. The Bible says in Gen 2:24 KJV, *"Therefore shall a man leave his father and his mother, and shall cleave unto his wife: and they shall be one flesh."* Because of the sanctity of marriage, responsibilities shift for the husband and wife. The two leave their father and mother and join to become one flesh. Your immediate family is no longer your mother and father, sister or brother. They are now your extended family. Your immediate family, the family that God is now holding you accountable for, is your spouse and kids, if you have any. Everyone and everything else is no longer your responsibility and play second fiddle to your immediate family. You do not take from your immediate family's needs to fill the needs of others. You can however take from your surplus if you so desire, and with your spouse's permission, to help others in need. For clarification, your immediate family are the people who live under your roof and those whom you can legally claim are your dependents. This does not include grown siblings, aging parents, or your adult children.

Children

You may have heard the saying, "When they're young they sit on your lap but when they're old they sit on your heart." This is the case with children and it is so easy to give to them but some parents have an unhealthy giving pattern when it comes to their offspring. Some parents feel guilty for the mistakes they made in raising their children and other parents think it's their fault where their adult children are in life so they give their child whatever they want to ease their own conscience, but whether you raised them right or not, parents are not responsible for their child's poor choices. You don't have to give money to get your child out of a jam or make it easier for them to overcome the consequences of bad decisions. You must remember you are not the first parent to have your children go wrong even though you've taught them correctly and steered them in the right direction. Who was the first parent to have this disappointment? God was.

As told in Genesis 1:27-30, God made every provision for the first man and woman on Earth, yet they decided to listen to another's voice. Adam and Eve were cared and provided for. They had no worries. Their world was perfect! They only had one thing they were not supposed to do, yet despite all of God's provisions, warnings, and instruction, Adam and Eve did the unthinkable and sinned against God. God's first "children" blew it. Now if Adam and Eve can go against a perfect Father, what makes you think that your children won't go against an imperfect parent, you? Do you think you are better than God? If His children disappointed Him, who makes no mistakes and is perfect in all His ways, what makes you think that your children won't disappoint you? Do you think God is to blame for Adam and Eve's choices? No, of course He isn't. They made their choices despite all the love God showed them. Despite all the things He told them they could do, they carry out the one thing He told them not to do. So if God is not responsible for Adam and Eve's bad choices, then you also are not responsible for your adult children's choices. They are responsible. Just like God shut Adam and Eve out of the only home they knew, the Garden of Eden, so do you have the responsibility to shut your adult kids out of your home, your decision-making, and your pocketbook. Just like Adam and Eve had to endure the hardships and learnings of their bad choices, so your own children must succumb to the lessons due to the choices they have made. God didn't even give Adam and Eve a chance to mess up again. He kicked them out of the garden after they sinned just one time. We're actually more lenient on our kids when, even though it may not be a sin, we give them chance after chance after each poor financial choice they make.

Parents, when your children are adult age, or approaching adulthood, do not bail them out of their financial situations. (This applies to everyone in your life, not just your children.) If you do decide to bail them out, make it perfectly clear to them that you are doing it just this once, and that you hope they've learned their lesson, if not they are on their own. If you keep coming to their rescue, you are enabling them to continue the same behavior, this is not helping them or you.

Never Co-sign

If your precious one's car gets repossessed, do not try to get them out of the situation by co-signing for another car. Do not co-sign on anything for anyone nor for any reason—apartment leases, bank loans, wedding rings, for your children, best friend, parents, grandparents, nothing and no one.

When you co-sign, you are giving your name in pledge of another. Parents, do not think that because you signed your name, that your kids will respect your name or you being their parent, and pay their bills on time to protect you. It's not going to happen. If your kids have bad credit, they will destroy yours too if you let them. The creditors even know that. That goes for friends, relatives, and anyone else. Why do you think they don't qualify for that loan on their own? The finance company has looked at their credit report and has seen derogatory information on it that makes it a risk to loan them money. If a financial institution doesn't deem them worthy or trust they will get their money back, you probably will not get yours back either. It amazes me that people are willing to put their reputation on the line for someone who has already destroyed their own reputation. Do you think that anyone will respect your name over their own? So if they mess their own name up, yours will be next in line.

Do not be a man who strikes hands in pledge or puts up security for debts; if you lack the means to pay, your very bed will be snatched from under you. Proverbs 22:26-27 NIV

Most people who co-sign probably do not even look at the person's credit report that they are about to put their name and money on the line for. Why? They feel that would be rude or intrusive, yet they are willing to be intruded on. How crazy is that! If you are considering taking on someone else's debt, you should at least look at their credit report to see what their track record is and their habits when borrowing money. And get your mind made up that you probably will end up paying for the loan.

Back to your kids. You have already spent 18 years teaching and molding your children into what they should be. Parents are the most influential people in their children's life so if you have taught your kids how to handle money, then they should handle it well. The concerning thing however is the reality that you teach them the most by them watching you. No matter what you have told them, they will gravitate to what they see over what they hear. It is amazing how children copy their parents. My daughter Mariah received a toy cell phone as a gift. I thought it was cute and watched her talk on it at home but then she wanted to take it with her everywhere. She started talking on it in the car and wanted to take it in the store. I realized she was only doing what she had seen me do. And it was then that I knew I needed to tone it down and talk less. I was not being a good role model for her in this regard. Now if you were not a good role model as far as money goes, please level with your children and let them know about the mistakes, I mean bad choices, you have made.

Don't act like you haven't made mistakes. Admit to your children that you mismanaged money and if necessary, tell them that you are not a good financial example for them to follow. Show them specifics of how and on what you messed up on. It's O.K. It is better for them to learn from your mistakes than for them to repeat the same. It may have taken you five years to recover, but it may take them ten years if they repeat or make worse choices than you did.

You are still a good parent. Your kids already know you are not perfect. I do not know why parents try to shield their kids from their own shortcomings and mistakes. Stop acting like you did everything right and share with your kids what you did wrong, so they will not keep repeating the same mistakes. This is probably the reason why each generation gets more and more intelligent yet more dumb and farther away from God than the previous generation, because we as parents, grandparents, aunts, and uncles are too busy trying to cover up our faults that we don't pass down anything of value to the next generation. One of the best things you can do is tell someone the truth about how you messed up, so they can avoid the same or clean up their own mess. That's not mean. You are teaching them character. They will definitely appreciate the lesson more and will be less likely to repeat a bad decision when they are the ones that have to clean it up. A lesson is learned twice as fast when you have to clean it up yourself.

Two examples make this point clear—a teen mother and fish. Think of the teen mother who now has two kids because she was given too much help with the first one. She has parents who didn't want her to miss out on her childhood so they shielded her from the harsh realities of being a mother. They kept the child so the mom could go to every school activity. They bought the baby everything the baby needed and wanted and didn't require the mother or father to get any type of job to provide for the baby. Excuses were made for the teens instead and inevitably baby number two soon arrived. The teen parents think it's easy and will never get the full effect of being a parent because their parents took on most of *their* responsibilities.

I like the fish story, the second example. Many of you have heard that if you give a man a fish, he'll eat for a day, but if you teach him how to fish, he'll eat for a lifetime. This is so true with your own children. Teach them how to be responsible for their actions regarding money. If you keep bailing them out, they will never learn and they'll probably take you down with them. Sometimes people are in the shape they are in because God has allowed a curse to come over their money, sometimes due to disobedience as you saw in the previous chapter, and nothing *you* do will break the curse. Until that person gets right with God and does right, the curse will remain. If you continue to give to this person, not only will their situation not get better, it will drain your resources as well. Another drain on your resources is giving to someone who mismanages money. When you see someone making poor choices, giving them money only allows the poor choices to continue. There is no change in behavior. It is just like giving an alcoholic a drink when you know they haven't managed their drinking. They will only mismanage what you give them, when you could have used the money for yourself.

Most of the time, people have to get themselves out of the mess they have made in order for real change to take place. This may take time, much more time than what they want, and probably require more money to do, but the lesson is learned during that time and with their resources. *They* are actually changed during the process.

Another way of looking at this is to examine the life of a caterpillar. In order to change into a butterfly, the caterpillar must spend some time isolated in a sac called a chrysalis. Once the sac breaks open, the butterfly must get *itself* out of the sac in order for its wings to function correctly. The wings get their strength from the butterfly's struggle of freeing itself from the sac. If someone or something was to help the butterfly get out of the sac, its wings would not be functional. Although the help would allow the butterfly to avoid or shorten the temporary struggle, the help would also cause long-term consequences for the butterfly's growth and development. Like the caterpillar, many of us must struggle through the sac, the financial lesson, without aid from another, so we can financially soar with our own strong wings.

Knowledge

One thing you can give your children is knowledge. Teach your children about money while they are young and make the effort to continue giving them teachable moments throughout their childhood.

Train up a child in the way he should go: and when he is old, he will not depart from it. Proverbs 22:6 KJV.

You normally hear this passage of scripture during youth services at church but this scripture applies to all aspects of training a child so they will be well equipped as adults. Train them to set priorities, respect authority, abide by rules, accept consequences, provide for their families, and everything else they need to know, including money.

Training is more than telling your child a few times what to do. Training is telling what, why, and how to do something. Training is showing how to do something and also observing the person trying to learn and implement what you are teaching them, and you must alter your training based on each child. One child may catch on fast, the other slow. When they mess up, you are to show them where they went wrong and how to fix it. You know they have it down when they continually do the process correctly. And you know they have mastered it when they begin to train others.

Think about how you are trained at work. You may be given a book or manual to read, you may have to go to classes, take a series of tests to show you have learned individual sections, or endure on-the-job training. Well, parents have the unique challenge of being life-long trainers to their children but if you wait until your children are teenagers before you start teaching them about money, you've waited too late. They will be much more equipped when you start young. Four, five, and six year olds should know what tithing is. This helps parents leave a legacy of spiritual and financial knowledge to their children.

A good man leaveth an inheritance to his children's children: and the wealth of the sinner is laid up for the just. Proverbs 13:22 KJV

This verse not only applies to money itself but also what to do with the money. If you never teach your children what to do with money, never give them an example to hand down to their children, the financial inheritance that you do leave will be used up by ignorance and negligence. Your grandchildren will either pilfer their inheritance, or your adult children will find a way to spend all the money before anything ever gets to your grandchildren.

What do most of us do when our children get money from relatives or friends for occasions such as birthdays and Christmas? We give it to them and take them to the store and let them spend it all on a toy or whatever else they want. Well, what about teaching them early about the importance of saving and investing their money? We need to ask them first of all, how much are you going to give to God's kingdom? Then, how much are you going to save, invest, and spend?

Get your kids a purse or a wallet and give them four jars or envelopes—one for God, one for savings, one for investing, and one for spending. Guide them to give at least 10%, save 10%, invest 10%, and spend some of the rest. Use the investing jar or envelope as age appropriate. Choose a specified time when you go to the bank and let your kids deposit their own money.

Go through the drive-thru or let them go inside and walk up to the teller because it is more powerful when they do it themselves. They need to know that the money is theirs and that it is their responsibility. I can't tell you how empowering this is for a child. Just watch their faces light up each time they see their accounts grow.

What an awesome principle you would be teaching your kids at a young age. You also have to be careful that you do not insist that they save everything someone has given them since this may plant a seed that money is not to be enjoyed. You want them to have a balance. You want them to give, save, and spend their money on whatever they want to spend it on. You will be teaching your children principles which is much more effective than just telling them.

Since your child is a minor, their account will be tied to yours so here are a few cautions. Do not touch your child's money for any reason—not to cover your own bills, to tie you over 'till payday, to pay for their school activity fees or their lunch money. These are your responsibility. Do not have their account tied to yours as an overdraft protection, meaning that if your personal account is overdrawn the bank will automatically take the overdrawn money out of your child's account. Don't justify it saying you will replace it and it doesn't matter because you're taking care of them every day, not even if you were the one who initially funded the account. That is a bad habit to start and it is hard to keep up with how much you are taking out of your child's account versus how much you are putting back in. Besides, that's why you have your own emergency fund.

Once your kid sees their balance grow, they will want to continue that trend and will start asking you about ways they can earn money, among other things, so below are a few additional ideas on how to teach your children about money:

- Reward their good report card grades with cash ($5 for each A, $2 for B's, $1 for E's and $0.50 for S's)
- Encourage them to sell candy to help pay for their uniform (even though you may have already paid for it)
- Have a lemonade stand
- Clip coupons
- When you grocery shop let them pick out the best values
- Go through the self check line and let them scan some groceries and notice how much items cost
- Give them the grocery receipt and let them examine it
- Have them calculate their own tithes
- Share your household bills with them. Let them actually see the bills so they know how much the light bill is, water bill, cell phone, etc.
- Let them earn money by doing certain age-appropriate household chores.
- Take them to the dollar store. Give them a dollar and let them buy one thing. Then when they don't have enough for the purchase give them the change to pay for it and explain to them how sales tax works.

Adolescence

At the age of 9 and 7 years old, our children already know that they are paying for their own vehicle if they want one. We will pay half of what they save up to buy the vehicle...a cash car. Is this child abuse? No, of course not. We just want our kids to value a high-ticket item such as a car. Now when I was a senior in high school my dad bought me my first car, an '81 four-door Honda Accord. I was so happy. Thank you, Daddy! Did he make me pay half for it? No, but I grew up differently than my kids. I didn't have any money saved up at that time. It would have been a shock for him to tell me at that point that I had to pay half for my vehicle when I had never been trained to do so.

Whatever life lessons you instill in your children, make sure you don't just spring it on them all of a sudden. You want to set them up for success by setting and communicating the expectations early. If you have a child in high school who is expecting you to buy their car, it may be a shock to suddenly inform them that they must pay the lion's share of it. Even if you are footing the whole bill, you still want them to appreciate the value of their own transportation so instead of buying a teenager a new vehicle, get them a cash car. A cash car is a car that you pay cash for. It may be a four thousand dollar car that doesn't look the best but they will appreciate it. Do not co-sign, you save up the money and get them the cash car. Of course they want a new car, who doesn't? Even as a young adult they think that's what they need but it's not. I know many people want to have their kids establish their credit by financing a car but again the Bible shows you are training them to be a life-long servant. You need to start them on the right foot with no debt. By the way, have you seen the cost of insurance for a young adult that drives a new car?

Relationships

A parent and child relationship is one that can be affected by money but let's look at others. Let me speak to the ladies for a moment. I think we as women like to come to the rescue. We are nurturers by nature so we like to make sure everyone is O.K. We don't like to see others in pain so we sacrifice to see them happy. We will actually put *ourselves* in pain to ease the pain of others. Please let this next statement resonate with you. You can't help everyone and you cannot help someone if you can't help yourself. As a woman it is not your responsibility to help your man, your boyfriend, your boo. Sound harsh? Listen to me carefully. Men are created differently than us. They are designed to be the priest, protector, and provider of their households. (Thank you Pastor Donald Powell Sr.) Providing is giving. If you are in a relationship, the man should be taking care of, providing for, and giving to you, the woman. The very makeup of a man's body structure was made to give, and the woman to receive. The man gives seed (in marriage of course) and the woman receives his seed.

Men also have a hunter's mentality. They can go out and "hustle" to make it. Anytime your man is asking *you* for money, it's a problem. That is a reversal of roles. Now *you* have become the provider. If you allow it, he will continue and you will keep doing it. Some men are slick piranhas waiting on their prey. Before you know it, he'll move in with you using the excuse that it's to save money or not wanting to uproot your kids, just any 'ol excuse. Before long, he'll lose his job and you'll be supporting him. Don't laugh, this has happened to many unsuspecting women. When you get fed up and tell him to leave, he'll send you on a guilt trip about you turning your back on him when he's down. Once these piranhas have stuck their sharp teeth into your finances, they'll leave you for another fish in the sea. I've seen many variations of this so beware if the male you are dating asks you for money. (He's not a man, he's a male, because men do not ask women for money.)

When you are in a courtship, and even before that, the man is pursuing you. Let him. The whole purpose of dating is to see if this person is the one you should marry so your main focus is to determine if this person is right for you. Women, the man is supposed to pursue you, not the other way around. That is how God designed it. As soon as you take the first step and ask the man out, you have just reversed both of your roles. Sound old fashioned? Well, the Bible says in Proverbs 18:22 NIV, *He who finds a wife finds what is good and receives favor from the Lord.*

The scripture doesn't say she who finds a husband. So women, it is not your job to look for a husband, so stop. You stay busy doing the Lord's work and making sure you are prepared for God's timing. Work on you and make sure you are striving to be the woman God desires.

Back to dating…When I was dating my husband, I did not pay for anything. Not one date did I ever pay for anything. Why? My decision was partly because I was more cautious due to the fact that I did not want to be taken advantage of as in a previous relationship. I did not really even notice I had done this until years later, after we were married, my husband jokingly brought it to my attention. If the man you are dating can't afford or will not make the sacrifice to spend enough money for a dinner and a movie, or whatever on you, then how will he afford to take care of you in a marriage? You are his first priority. A husband is supposed to be the provider and you *his* helper, not the other way around.

The LORD God said, "It is not good for the man to be alone. I will make a helper suitable for him." Genesis 2:18 NIV

Men, you do not have to spend money each time you are with her, but if you are not willing to spend money on this woman, then either you are not ready to be a husband (provider) or you are just not willing to spend your money on *her*. If that is the case, she is not the one for you.

Speaking of the roles of men and women even while dating, let me share what happened to me. Wait let me stop right there. I just got convicted. This did not just happen to me. I was not a passive player in this. I simply made bad, very bad choices. That "happened to me" statement is what a lot of women use to make it sound like we were a victim. We are not victims. We simply made bad choices and we should own up to them.

Yes, we were taken advantage of but, we allowed it and we need to take responsibility for our actions. If you would be honest, you would say that God did show you signs and warned you all along the way, but you, like me, did not take heed to it. You can say we were blinded by love or emotions, but we really just made the decision to ignore the warning signs.

Here is an example of not what happened to me, but what I let happen to me, what I allowed to happen. I tried my best to help a man I was dating when I was young (and naïve). He always was in one jam after another and I was the one he would run to. He used me because I let him. I actually thought I was being nice and that he was just running into a lot of bad situations due to a bad economy. The sad thing is that I did not have the money to help him but because of my love for him I made the foolish decision of taking out cash advances on my credit cards to help him pay his car note and whatever else he said he needed.

Every time he needed money, he had what seemed like a legitimate need. He even said we would go into business together, another gimmick that I gave him money for. It got so bad that my credit cards were maxed out. He even convinced me that if I got a loan from the bank that would help. I thank God for closing that door because I did unbelievably ask the bank for a loan, which they denied because of my high debt-to-income ratio. After it was all said and done, I had given this man $24,000. No, this is not a type-o. Yes, this is one of the most stupid things I have ever done. I share this because I don't want you to fall into the same financial trap. Don't feel guilty for saying, "No."

> *It takes a love for people to give your testimony and succumb yourself to the judgment of others just for the chance to help one person avoid what you went through or to give hope to that one person that they can overcome what they are going through, even if they are too ashamed to ever let you know.*
>
> **— Shalonda McFarland**

Don't ever say what you won't do. I was blinded by love, I mean I ignored the warning signs. It's usually the people you do the most for that mess over you the quickest. It's important to keep your sanity, your values, and morals. Do not get lost in love. You must be sure of what you stand for or love will make you fall for anything. I let love overpower my own common sense.

> It's been said, "There's a thin line between love and hate" but there is a huge gap between give and take.
> **—Shalonda McFarland**

Never *borrow* money to help someone else or loan anyone money that you need. It's O.K. to loan out of your surplus if you so desire, but not out of your need or guilt for that matter. I do not care whether it is a family member, close friend, co-worker, or someone on the street with a sign, do not give out of guilt.

Never get lax and think you have time so it's O.K. to loan someone money now because you won't need it until a few days or a few weeks from now. I loaned someone hundreds of dollars. They said they would give it back to me in one week. It took them 3 months to give me half of the money back that I loaned them. I still have not gotten the other half back. If you were in this situation and needed that money to pay a bill, what would you do? What would you do if you were the one who borrowed the money? Loaning money can destroy relationships so if you can't pay a friend back when you said you would, just be honest and tell them. If you can't pay it back at all, just say so. Don't ignore them or pretend you don't remember they loaned you money by not ever mentioning it again.

Money is blamed for a lot of things but it's actually the misuse of money and irresponsible people that's to blame. What people do with money, their actions, that's to blame. Money can be used for good or evil. When money is in a Christian's hands it's blessed money, and when it is in an evil person's hands, it's evil money. It all depends on who possesses it and what the use is for.

Marriage

Money issues are the number one reason for divorce. Before you decide to get married you need to know everything you can about this person you are going to spend the rest of your life with. Before you get married you need to look at his credit report, and he yours. I'm serious. You need to see what your soul mate's character is and one way to see his financial character is through a credit report. You need to talk about the positive and negative things on the report. Don't be scared to ask. You are about to be one with this person so you have a right to know; you must know. Why should an employer know his credit score and you don't? Why should a stranger in the finance office of a car dealership know his credit history and you, who will be with him for the rest of his life, not know? Everything on that report will affect you once you say, "I do." What if he has $7,000 of back child support on it, which by the way is accumulating 14% interest? You will not be buying a house anytime soon. Please do not be naive. Do your homework.

I am sending you out like sheep among wolves. Therefore be as shrewd as snakes and as innocent as doves. Matthew 10:16 NIV

Before my husband and I got married, I told him about the debt I had incurred due to my previous relationship. (I don't remember how much I had paid down before we had this talk.) I explained to him that this was unusual behavior for me and that I knew better than to let it happen. He told me some things about his past too.

That open and honest communication works wonders for a relationship. Not only do you need to research their financial history, but every aspect of this person. Are they a person of character? Are they giving or are they always trying to get over on someone and joke about it to you? It will not be long before *you* are their next joke. Sometimes we do more research on the company we want to work for than we do on our potential life-long spouse. Feel like a private investigator? Good, you need to since 90% of your quality of life will result from who you marry.

Christians versus Church Folk

Are they a Christian or do they just go to church? Does this question surprise you? Oh yes, not everyone that goes to church is a Christian. There are many people, male and female, who go to church for different reasons, some of which have nothing to do with Christ. There are those whose purpose is to lure the people that are in church away from church or to take advantage of who they feel is easy prey. Surprisingly, there are also people in positions at church who are not living as Christians. They know what to say and what not to say in church to fit in but their lifestyle is far from Him.

> *Beware of false prophets, which come to you in sheep's clothing, but inwardly they are ravening wolves.* Matthew 7:15 KJV

How is it possible that evil people could be in church? Why would God allow such people who have no plans to seek Him, to come into the midst of His people only to prey on them? I do not know the answer to that question but allowing this access is nothing new. Even Satan himself was allowed access, to come and go, in and out of heaven.

> *Now there was a day when the sons of God came to present themselves before the L*ORD*, and Satan came also among them. And the L*ORD *said unto Satan, Whence comest thou? Then Satan answered the L*ORD*, and said, From going to and fro in the earth, and from walking up and down in it.* Job 1:6-7 KJV

Just as he can come and go as he pleases, there are people in churches today that do the same, but they miss out on their own blessings because they're too busy trying to take the blessings of others. One of the first things they do is covet. At the root of covetousness is ungratefulness and a sense of entitlement. Even though "Do not covet" is the last of the Ten Commandments, it sums up the sixth through ninth, which actions are a result of coveting. (Exodus 20:17) Coveting is a matter of the heart and can lead to the action of murder, adultery, stealing, giving false testimony, etc. Some covet what other people have, meaning they don't trust God enough to believe He will bless them with something or someone of their own. They doubt God possibly because they know their heart is not right toward Him and they are not fully committed to God.

They seek His hand but deny His face, for they only want the blessing, not The Blesser. They may want Jesus as a Savior but reject Him as Lord over their life.

There are yet still those who are Christians but they have some nasty ways. Some of you know exactly what I'm talking about. One can go to church for years and regrettably not imitate Christ in their actions. This shows that you can be standing on the premises but not taking hold of His promises.

But the fruit of the Spirit is love, joy, peace, patience, kindness, goodness, faithfulness, gentleness and self-control. Galatians 5:22-23 NIV

Things That Keep Us From Giving

I heard someone once say there are two types of people in this world, no not movers and shakers, givers and takers. Givers give generously and takers take liberally. How do people know you are a Christian? Is it what you say or how you act? It's how you act, your lifestyle.

These people honor me with their lips, but their hearts are far from me. Matthew 15:8 NIV

A person can tell you they love you but their speech must line up with their actions. I heard the following on the radio, "If you were on trial for being a Christian, would there be enough evidence to convict you?" We need to be examples of Christ to all since we are the only Bible some people will ever read. Sadly some people won't even think to open up the book because they are turned off by the cover—our facial expressions, our attitudes and negative demeanors. Some so called Christians are the very ones who are preventing others from coming to Christ.

Don't be like the Pharisees and Sadducees whom John the Baptist called vipers in Matthew 3:7 and in Matthew 23:25 whom Jesus said, "You hypocrites, you clean the outside of the cup but leave the inside dirty." Unlike hypocrites, we should be pleasant and courteous, actually Christ-like. Unfortunately there are some who continually exhibit non Christian behaviors. Do you find yourself practicing these behaviors? Rolling your eyes? Always speaking negative? Being stingy? Cursing people out? Looking down on others? Acting holier than thou? Is that a good witness? These behaviors are not giving, but taking. A person's behavior stems from their attitude and your attitude is a reflection of your mind, will, and emotions, which is your soul and the Bible declares, "Beloved, I wish above all things that thou mayest prosper and be in health, even as thy soul prospereth." 3 John 1:2 KJV. So you can't expect to prosper without first getting your soul right. You are either a giver or a taker, you can't be both just as you can't have blessings and cursings coming out of the same mouth.

Out of the same mouth come praise and cursing. My brothers, this should not be. James 3:10 NIV

You either give love or hate, give others happiness or sorrow. You're either a good witness or a bad witness for Christ. This doesn't mean we should just take whatever someone throws at us. We're not to be doormats. You can still speak your mind, still be firm, and still hold people accountable, all while being a Christian. Attitudes that can hinder your giving are jealousy, pride, envy, and coveting. Jealousy, which we touched on in the Faith chapter, is not wanting someone to have what they have because you feel you deserve it more, pride (conceit) is having an exaggerated opinion of yourself, envy is being resentful toward a person because of what they have, and coveting is desiring what belongs to someone else.

When you are jealous, you feel entitled. You may have a wealthy relative or friend and you will stop speaking to them and say they've changed, but really it's you who have shown your true colors and are jealous of their success. You did not make the sacrifices they made, or take the risk they did to get where they are. They have a right to enjoy the fruits of their labor without people having a fit over their success. People may want you to succeed but they don't want you to be too successful. I know there are some people who forget who helped them get where they are today but you've got to let God handle that. We don't trust God enough to provide for us so we try and make ourselves feel good by tearing someone else down. This does not have to be. There are enough blessings to go around for everyone. Heaven does not have a shortage of blessings. I like the way Reverend Eric Cortez Sr. explains it, "When you have a need, nobody's in heaven panicking, saying 'What we gonna do?'" There is no lack in heaven, no shortage of God's supply.

Peter fairly exploded with his good news: "It's God's own truth, nothing could be plainer: God plays no favorites! It makes no difference who you are or where you're from—if you want God and are ready to do as he says, the door is open... Acts 10:34 The Message

God is not a respecter of persons which means what He will do for you, He will do for me. We pray

"Our Father" not "My Father." Because He's more than just my or your father, He will bless me *and* you for we are all His children. But He will not give you more than you can handle. If you look down on others because you earn $30,000, why would He allow you to earn $60,000? You can't handle it. How much do you think you will get from God with an attitude of ingratitude?

If you have examined your thoughts and attitudes and realize that you have been acting with jealousy, envy, strife, covetousness, etc. you can change with God's help. Ask Him to help you have a healthy view of other people. How do you do this? There are many ways. You can start by simply giving genuine compliments or trying to get to know a person better but the best way to have a healthy view of someone is to pray for them. Yes, pray for them, even when you feel they don't deserve it. Just as the Bible says to pray for your enemies, you should pray for those you currently feel jealous of. How can you stay jealous of someone you are constantly praying for?

> *Ye have heard that it hath been said, Thou shalt love thy neighbour, and hate thine enemy. But I say unto you, Love your enemies, bless them that curse you, do good to them that hate you, and pray for them which despitefully use you, and persecute you; that ye may be the children of your Father which is in heaven: for he maketh his sun to rise on the evil and on the good, and sendeth rain on the just and on the unjust.* Matthew 5:43-45 KJV

When you do this you are exemplifying God's character. Note the text didn't say love what your enemies do but to love the enemy. Now this does not mean you are to just accept any wrong that is done to you. You are not a punching bag. God does not want you to be in a harmful situation. Some circumstances will require you pray and forgive but end a relationship to get out of harm's way. And in a less dire situation, this doesn't mean you have to hang out with this person but loving them will keep you at peace and allow room for God's vengeance. He can repay them better than you can. (Romans 12:19)

Be ye therefore merciful, as your Father also is merciful. Judge not, and ye shall not be judged: condemn not, and ye shall not be condemned: forgive, and ye shall be forgiven: Give, and it shall be given unto you; good measure, pressed down, and shaken together, and running over, shall men give into your bosom. For with the same measure that ye mete withal it shall be measured to you again. Luke 6:36-38 KJV

I know this may sound crazy and totally backward, but that is sometimes how God seems to us. A lot of the time, what he tells us to do does not make sense. This may not be the easiest thing to do, but when you change your thoughts, you change your words and actions. You then form new habits which changes your character. As Pastor Chris Welch says, "Your character can reverse your condition."

Takers

Are you a giver or a taker? Here are some common situations you may be guilty of that may mean you are a taker. These actions will not only hinder your blessings, but can also place a curse on your finances. The following are simply symptoms of the taker disease.

Example #1: Are you talking about the man or woman of God? God said in Deut 28:7 that he'd handle your enemies and in Exodus he showed through the leprosy of Miriam that he would curse them that curse you and bless them that bless you. God has cursed some of you because you have cursed others. Some of you are always shooting down God's anointed, and are simultaneously placing a curse over your own selves. Keep your mouth off of the preacher and other Christians.

Example #2: There are many women that are stopping their children from seeing their fathers because the man is no longer part of the woman's life. There is a void in the child's life that only their own father can fill. No matter how much you disagree or don't get along with the father, it's not your child's problem. Children are innocent and did not ask to come here. You are taking their childhood away.

Here are some games some "Christian" women play when it comes to their children seeing their fathers. They:

- Move as far away from the father as possible to make it harder for him to see his child consistently.
- Disregard court-ordered visitation and will not let the father see the child. Some mothers will send their children to live with relatives before they will let the child live with their biological father.

- Deny the father of seeing the child if the father is a few minutes late picking the child up or dropping the child off.
- Talk bad about the father. I'm not talking about letting the child know what happened between you two or why you're no longer together, but tearing your ex down with your words and telling your son that his father is a "no good such and such" is not healthy for the child. After all, he had to have been good in some kind of way or you wouldn't have had a child with him right?

There are many more instances but the point is the woman goes out of her way to try and find a fault, mistake, or loophole in the system to take as much from the man she used to love. The irony of this is these are probably the same ones that will file for an increase in child support money when they aren't even holding up their end of the court order, let alone using the child support for the child. These women are so focused on hurting the man that they don't see that they're hurting their child the most. These mothers take advantage of the biased court system which will mostly favor the woman, unless she is severely unfit. If you are a woman, or a man playing these type of games, you are a taker and you need to examine your motives and actions. You are hurting the child and yourself, whether you realize it or not.

We don't trust God enough to do what He says, instead we have the same actions as the world.

Example #3: Another situation that shows you are a taker is stealing. Some people steal from the company they work for, stealing time and resources from their employer. They cheat on time sheets, call someone to clock them in, and take supplies and equipment for their own personal use. They will use the excuse that they aren't being paid what they're worth so they can justify their actions. Stop taking what doesn't belong to you and find a job that does pay you what you are worth.

You also have some people who steal from the church in what some would call "little ways." They are taking church resources for their own personal use. You have trustees who are taking money out of the offering plate and stuffing it under their sleeves. You have pastors who are using the church funds for their own extended family, not to grow the kingdom.

You have some parents who are using their kids' identity to open accounts for credit cards, light bills, etc. Not only is this immoral, it is illegal. They are stealing their child's identity and future and the child is paying for the parent's bad choices. This is a selfish act.

There are also Christians who try and swindle others, they try to get over, and want something for nothing, something for free. How can a Christian be a taker? That is a good question. Just because you are a Christian doesn't mean you don't have to follow the rules, don't have to pay the same price as others. Some people who say they are Christians try to take advantage of situations. You have husbands taking advantage of their wives, adult children taking advantage of their aging parents, deacons, ministers, and even some pastors taking advantage of "their" members. When you take, you are only hindering yourself. I've heard it explained this way, you should be a river not a reservoir. A river has a steady flow and a reservoir is stagnant. A river gives life and is a channel. A reservoir continues to receive or take what flows in, never giving back, and since there's no outlet it promotes death. We should be rivers not reservoirs. Blessings should flow through us freely like a river. We should not hoard things like a reservoir.

> *You can't give or receive with a clenched hand.*
> **—Shalonda McFarland**

Some people just try to get over on others and are dishonest in their dealings. Some people foolishly spend or waste their money then want to ask for what others have. They are takers. Like the five foolish virgins in the 25th chapter of Matthew who ran out of oil because they didn't bring enough, people will have the audacity to use up their money and then try and get your surplus. They spend their money on what they want to spend it on, and when it's gone they look to you. Some people live their whole lives acting irresponsibly and reckless. They drink up, party up, or shop up their money and then expect others to come to their rescue. If you give of yours, both of you will be in lack. Everyone has the same opportunity to make good financial choices.

You are also probably a taker if you:

- Take advantage of a person and pay them less than the agreed upon price, or simply nothing at all.
- Blow your money off or spend it unwisely then come ask the church to help you with your bills.

- Trash your apartment because you were evicted, destroy your house because you were foreclosed on, or deface your car because it was repossessed.

> *The church is not a safety net for your bad choices.*
> **—Shalonda McFarland**

If you are a taker, please examine why you are and make the necessary changes to line your life up with God's word. If your hand is always closed because you're steady taking from others, God can't bless you or anyone else through you.

How To Be A Good Witness

There are also subtle ways we can take from others and may not even realize it. Barbara Ehrenreich, in her book *Nickel and Dimed* gives her account of the worse tippers, which she notes are Christians. "The worst for some reason are the visible Christians. Like the ten person table, all jolly and sanctified after Sunday night's service, who run me mercilessly and then leave me $1 on a $92 bill; or the guy with the crucifixion T-shirt, someone to look up to, who complains that his baked potato is too hard, and his iced tea too icy, I cheerfully fix both, and leaves no tip at all. As a general rule, people wearing crosses or WWJD, what would Jesus do buttons, look at us disapprovingly no matter what we do, as if they were confusing waitressing with Mary Magdalene's original profession."

As sad as that sounds, I have been to restaurants with Christians that behave this way. I'm sure you have too. You hope that the order is right so they won't "act up." Now to be fair, non-Christians act this way too but it is a terrible witness for a Christian to behave in such a way, where nothing you do will satisfy them, or being too demanding or harsh with your waitress. The customer is *not* always right.

So in everything, do to others what you would have them do to you, for this sums up the Law and the Prophets. Matthew 7:12 NIV

As we have therefore opportunity, let us do good unto all men, especially unto them who are of the household of faith. Galatians 6:10 KJV

Things to Remember

- Oxygen masks in airplanes
- Adam and Eve
- Teach a man to fish
- Butterfly analogy
- Parent trainers
- Teen mom
- Piranhas
- River vs reservoir

More Giving Scriptures

Do not be deceived: God cannot be mocked. A man reaps what he sows. Galatians 6:7 NIV

For even when we were with you, we gave you this rule: "If a man will not work, he shall not eat." 2 Thessalonians 3:10 NIV

And the King shall answer and say unto them, Verily I say unto you, Inasmuch as ye have done it unto one of the least of these my brethren, ye have done it unto me. Matthew 25:40 KJV

Many will say to me in that day, Lord, Lord, have we not prophesied in thy name? and in thy name have cast out devils? and in thy name done many wonderful works? And then will I profess unto them, I never knew you: depart from me, ye that work iniquity. Matthew 7:22-23 KJV

*So behave properly, as people do in the day. Do not go to wild parties or get drunk or be vulgar or indecent. Do not quarrel or be **jealous**.* Romans 13:13 Contemporary English Version

Be not forgetful to entertain strangers: for thereby some have entertained angels unawares. Hebrews 13:2 KJV

For ye have the poor with you always, and whensoever ye will ye may do them good: but me ye have not always. Mark 14:7 KJV

But ye shall receive power, after that the Holy Ghost is come upon you: and ye shall be witnesses unto me both in Jerusalem, and in all Judaea, and in Samaria, and unto the uttermost part of the earth. Acts 1:8 KJV

Those who sow in tears will reap with songs of joy. He who goes out weeping, carrying seed to sow, will return with songs of joy, carrying sheaves with him. Psalm 126:5-6 NIV

*Money does not change you,
it reveals you.*
—**Shalonda McFarland**

Chapter Four
Living Your Dreams

Nightmare on YOUR Street

Do you see a man skilled in his work? He will serve before kings; he will not serve before obscure men.
Proverbs 22:29 NIV

For the LORD God is a sun and shield: the LORD will give grace and glory: no good thing will he withhold from them that walk uprightly.
Psalm 84:11 KJV

We all have been asked as little children, "What do you want to be when you grow up?" This is such a simple yet empowering question to ask a child. The question itself is affirming to any child because it implies two things. One, we are not limited by choice but have the option of *choosing* anything in this world. We can dream big. And two, it implies we have the *ability* to be anything we want to be; or so we thought. Then we grow up and are faced with the reality that we do not have the skills of Michael Jordan, the voice of Whitney Houston, the talent of Michael Jackson, the words of Maya Angelou, nor the charisma of Oprah Winfrey. What on earth do we do now? Before you know it, we are adults. Some of us have graduated from college and are working in different fields than what our degrees are in or some of us have never gone to college and are just working at the first place that had an opening and met our minimum wage criteria. Yet others are making a lot of money by society's standard but hate to go to work each day. As we consider the paths we could have taken, the choices we should have made, and lost opportunities, we are left disappointed. Somehow our dreams have turned into nightmares.

So what do we do now? Do we lull ourselves into mediocrity while we continue on the "Thank God it's Friday, Oh, Lord it's Monday" pendulum? No, we need to take action and live the way God intended. God has placed unique gifts and talents inside each and every one of those he created; and it is our job to cultivate, refine, and put to use that which He gave us.

How do you know what your gifts are? Think about what you are naturally good at and what you love to do and would do even if you were never paid. What are you doing now that you love, that you have a passion for? Discover what you love to do, and you'll never have to work a day in your life. Why? Because you'll be having so much fun it won't feel like work. Find your calling in life, your purpose, what you were designed to do. It is true people succeed when they are doing what they are called to do. Embrace your passion even if it doesn't make sense or you can't see yourself making the money you want. For example, if you love teaching but feel you can't live on the average teacher's salary, look into nontraditional teaching jobs. Teaching is not limited to a classroom. A life coach and a manager both teach. One teaches an individual about certain aspects of life, the other teaches a group of people various processes within an organization. If you can't see how the money will come but teaching children is your calling, then just do what you love and the reward will come.

Don't put any limits on yourself or the paths you take, for there is no one written path to success. You can be a boxer, sell grills, write a book, and be a minister, all in one lifetime. Don't let someone put you in a box. Live your dream not others.

A man's gift maketh room for him, and bringeth him before great men. Proverbs 18:16 KJV

God has placed different gifts and talents in every person. Some people may have multiple gifts and talents, and do nothing with them, while those that have a single gift or talent may do more to cultivate it. However many gifts you have, develop them. Your gifts are normally in line with your desires so follow them. God gives desires to those who love him, and He equips us with everything we need to fulfill the purpose He has given us. I'm not saying you do not need others to fulfill your dreams, you absolutely do. Even with God's equipping, He places people in your life to teach, encourage, and position you to fulfill your purpose and make your dream a reality.

Need a little help discovering your calling? Write down at least three things that you love and would enjoy every day.

_____

_____

_____

If you haven't thought of anything you currently do, think back to the things that excited you when you were young. What were you passionate about during that time? Perhaps football, but you think you're too old or too slow or too whatever to play pro ball. O.K., maybe being a professional player isn't God's design or maybe that was God's perfect plan for your life and you chose a different plan. There may be many reasons why childhood dreams fade and we wake up one day regarding that dream as a nightmare because we only live that dream while we are asleep. You may have had an injury that hindered your dream, a parent that did not support your dream, or maybe you sabotaged your own dream. It's OK, God has a plan that you have not yet explored so be creative about how you can get paid to do what you are passionate about. You might have liked sports because of the competitiveness, the team mindset, or the detailed workout regime. Take the reasons you liked a particular thing and transfer that to a job that fits that description. If you need more details, there are many books on the subject. One such book is *48 Days To The Work You Love* by Dan Miller.

What has God placed on your heart? What keeps you up at night and keeps resurfacing in your mind? Please take action on it. If you do not use the gifts and talents God has given you, he will give it to someone else. If you do not live out your purpose and follow your dreams, you will either live miserable or die pregnant, never giving birth to your dreams. Are you pregnant with an idea, an invention, a song, a business? Birth the baby! Just as a woman gives birth to a natural baby, it is time that you give birth to your dreams and the gifts and talents that God has placed inside of you. I'm not saying it will be easy. Oh, I wish it was. If God gave you a dream, you'd think He'd make it easier to do His will but that may not be the case. You probably will have labor pains. But just as with a natural delivery, when the baby is birthed, you forget about the pain and enjoy the blessing. During the pain, God is testing you, not because he doesn't know what you will do, but to show *you* what you are capable of.

The problem we face when waiting for something to be birthed is The Wait. Sometimes it seems like forever for our dream to come to pass. We know God has gifted us and has promised us things but it seems like there is a blockage and then we question God, the promise, and our abilities. With a natural birth, it is easy to determine the due date. You might not know the exact date of the birth but you know within nine months, a baby is coming. Not so with birthing our gifts and talents and seeing the fruits of our labor. We don't know the time; it may be next month, next year, or even five years later before we see the birth so one can easily become frustrated when your best efforts seem only to produce delayed or unfulfilled promises, but keep going.

Have you forgotten how to dream? Do you remember what you love to do or have you forgotten? Let's explore. What do you have the knack for? What cause or organization pulls at your heartstring? Where do you volunteer? Do you love to coach little league? You already do it for free. You volunteer 20 hours a week already—you spend two hours twice a week for practice, the two hours on Saturday for games, the hour every night looking at the game footage, so why not get paid to do something you love? No, you say, that is my unwind time, if I were to get paid for it, I would no longer find it fun. Really? I beg to differ. No, you say that's only in the summer, what would I do the rest of the year? Well, you can transfer those skills to a similar opportunity. What about refereeing? The point is we will spend 83,200 hours of our lifetime working. That's if you only work 40 hour weeks and only work 40 years of your life, for instance starting at age 20 and retiring at age 60. If you work 50 hours a week, bump that up to 104,000 hours. That is a lot of hours and many years doing something you do not have a passion for, working at a job you may hate just to pay bills, bills, and more bills.

Here are a few more questions you may want to ask yourself to give your career search some direction.

- Do I have the passion for this career?
- Do I have the skills or talent for it?
- What are the educational requirements for this position?
- Does the position require additional degrees or any certifications?
- Does it also require job experience? If so, how many years?
- Can I get the job experience as an intern or on a volunteer basis?
- What is the average starting salary?
- What is the median pay and how does it vary by state?
- What other positions or job titles complement this one?
- What are normal working hours?
- What are the travel requirements? How often? Average length of trip?
- What is the average length of time in this position and/or field?

Ask the questions, do the due diligence. No one wants to expend resources to get somewhere only to discover that it's not what you thought it was. You don't want to go through medical school and then discover that you are nauseated by the sight of blood.

You don't want to enroll in aviator school only to discover you're afraid of heights. Dream big and live your dream in your career or entrepreneurial pursuits.

We must be careful not to be lulled into a routine of mediocrity that keeps us from change, due to our environment, what we are exposed to, or because we are scared to take a risk and drop "a safe job" to walk in faith.

Your Speech

Another way to live on purpose is to speak on purpose. Speaking on purpose means to not only speak words of affirmation on your own life, but to also be mindful of any negative words that come from your own lips and those spoken upon you by other people. Recall the lyrics to *Good Times*, a popular 70's TV show, which seem to suggest, even if we're just getting by, that we should be happy just to survive. I used to watch this show growing up and would recite the music by heart, not realizing the ramifications of what I was hearing and speaking through my own mouth.

A catchy opening to a great show but unfortunately it is a constant reminder of the cycle some of us have seen growing up, and have now found to be our everyday reality. This is not the way to live and is unacceptable for the believer. You owe it to yourself and your family to be the best and most-fulfilled *you* possible. It is not God's design, nor desire for you to survive, but to thrive. God wants to do more than you can ask or think, not just "meet a payment." He's made you the lender and not the borrower. He wants you to prosper, not just get you "out from under." He purposed for you to soar like an eagle, not just to "keep your head above water."

Live on purpose and be all He has designed for you to be.

Death and life are in the power of the tongue: and they that love it shall eat the fruit thereof. Proverbs 18:21 KJV

We should be mindful of the words we say because words are so powerful. What you think, you will say and what you say, you will do. Words give life. The heavens and the earth were created by God's words. When He said, "Let there be" he spoke creation into existence. Genesis 1:1-2:3 KJV

You must constantly speak positive words over yourself. These words need to be verbally spoken not just read silently from a piece of paper or recited in your mind alone. Those ways are good but you get more power from spoken words because not only is your mouth saying the positive things, but your brain is also processing the words that are coming from your mouth and attempting to make them come to pass. So for example, if you want to own your own business, you need to speak things as if they are, "I own my own construction company." The Bible tells us that speaking a thing is just as important as doing a thing so we should constantly speak life into our situation just as we work daily toward fulfilling our goals. What we speak, whether positive or negative, our mind starts to figure out a way to fulfill, then our actions start to mirror what our mind has figured out. How powerful are our words!

From the fruit of his lips a man is filled with good things as surely as the work of his hands rewards him. Proverbs 12:14 NIV

Start now and be consistent. Speak good over yourself and your entire family because not only do adults need this but children as well. One must constantly negate the negative words that are thrust upon us, as early as childhood, even as early as a baby in the womb. You've heard the subtle words that are thrust upon children:

- He's nosy
- That child is bad
- You're just like your father
- She's too skinny, she's too fat
- She's not good at math, etc.

You have to pump more positive into children to overcome the negative. The same with you, keep speaking positive over your life to overcome all the negative you've heard, even those planted in you from childhood that you may not even remember but your mind retained on a subconscious level, that you find yourself acting out.

Just like a scale you must continue to heap positive words on one side to offset the negative words that are constantly dropped on the other side, by others and by ourselves. Here are some negative things we sometimes say to ourselves without knowing it and some examples of positive words we can start planting in our lives today.

Negative:

- I can't afford that
- I'm not a morning person
- I can't get going until I've had my coffee
- It doesn't matter what you do, they're all about

diversity so they're still going to promote a person of color or a woman over me
- It doesn't make a difference how good you are, I still have two strikes against me because I'm a minority and a woman
- Something always seems to come up

What you say doesn't even have to be true, you can speak good and bad things into existence. Don't talk your way out of a blessing. You can do the groundwork and get prepared for your dream and then self sabotage your work by thinking and talking your way out of it at the same time. When you say negative things, it plants seeds in your mind which start to grow and manifest itself in your actions. Whatever seeds you water and cultivate, that's the ones that will grow so water and cultivate the good seeds that have been planted in your mind.

Positive:

- I am a child of the King
- I am efficient and effective
- I make good choices
- I'm a valued employee
- I have unique ideas
- I manage my time well
- People like me and I am successful at all I endeavor
- God has placed good things in me
- I am perfectly created
- I am a man/woman of purpose
- People look up to me
- I do what I set my mind to
- I am creative and overflowing with ideas

- I am blessed so abundantly that I'm able to give back to others

Use these and add more or make up your own. I suggest writing these down on a piece of paper and place it in your purse or wallet, tape them to your mirror or bathroom door, place these in your top desk drawer at work, or record them on your cell phone and play it back in the morning on your commute to work. This way you'll also be able to recite the words with the recorded message.

In The Meantime

So you've discovered your calling and now you're getting ready to make the transition. But this is the test. What will you do in the meantime? What will you do while you wait for the promise? And what if you can't live your dreams this exact second? What do you do while preparing to start your business or land your dream job? Instead of giving up or complaining, we must have an attitude of expectancy, gratitude, and FAITH. The answer in short: honor God right where you are. Don't wait until you get the job you want, be a good witness of a hard, dependable worker right now. Act responsibly with the job you have now, and soon the career you want will appear. If you are effective where you are now, bigger and better opportunities will be presented to you. Remember the words of the master in the parable, The Word says if you are faithful over a few things, He will make you ruler over many. (Matthew 25:21)

How do you show faithfulness? Below is a list of characteristics of a good faithful worker:

- Honest (Integrity)
- Reliable
- Dependable
- Approachable
- Competent
- Positive Attitude
- Thorough
- Efficient
- Prompt
- Responsible
- Trustworthy
- Teachable
- Present

Keep preparing yourself. Do more, stretch yourself, and stay faithful so you'll be ready when opportunity comes.

What Keeps Us From The Next Level

In contrast, the attitudes and behavior we exhibit of an unfaithful worker keep us bound and limits our opportunities. Here are some characteristics:

- Gossiper
- Complainer
- Time-waster
- Inefficient
- Belief that just showing up means you are working
- Liar
- Blamer
- Negative Attitude

- Entitlement Mentality
- Wearing revealing clothes
- Unprofessional
- Flirtatious
- Unapproachable, or difficult to work with

These traits will keep you right where you are, or worse leave you out of a job. If you find yourself exercising these detrimental behaviors, you are either in the wrong job which is making you miserable or you are a miserable person turning a good job bad. Either way, you should make a change. Another attitude that keeps us from the next level is complacency. Sometimes we get stuck in our routines; we are sucked in by our habits and everyday rituals that we don't leave time for improvement in our professional or personal lives. Take steps in your spare time to help you move toward your dream. Invest time and resources in yourself. A few ways to do this are to go back to school to support a new career, or gain more exposure by volunteering for a project that gives you the opportunity to work cross functionally, or sign up for training classes that broaden your skill set.

In order for your dream to come into reality, you've got to dedicate some time beyond your regular duties. You don't think you have spare time? Oh really? Let's explore ways of finding time. First, think of where your time goes on a typical weekday, then Saturday and Sunday. Write down everything you do and how long it takes you to do it for each day. Let's start with the T.V. Do you watch a certain show every night? That's thirty minutes to an hour you can save. Do you watch the news two or three times a day? That's two to three hours you can save. Try watching the news every other day or listening to the news as you commute to and from work. Television is one of the biggest time wasters. Each time you turn the T.V. on, you probably will spend at least one hour watching it. Each movie you watch lasts about two hours. Are you addicted to soap operas? Do you have to watch every football game each season? Must you watch four game shows a night?

There are so many things that compete for our attention. Because we are faced with so many distractions today, we must take deliberate steps to stay focused. You will find the time and money for what you really want to do. You either spend time or invest time, spend money or invest money so when you are embarking on an activity, take this into consideration.

Now some of us have a hard time "finding time" because we spend too much time at our jobs. That's right. Some of us give too much time to our employers. We think working 60-80 hours a week is necessary for what our job title entails which leaves us no time for our families, ourselves, or our dreams. Some of us are not paid hourly, but are salaried, and are expected to get the job done without being paid any overtime. Yes, some of us are managers and are expected to work longer, but everything must be done in moderation. You could work all night and still find something else that needs to be done. No matter how much you do, you or someone else will still find more work and just because a person works longer hours doesn't mean they are more effective.

Some of us truly work long hours but if you're salaried, remember you still get paid for a 40-hour work week. Look at your paystub and let those 40 hours remind you that no matter how many hours you're putting in, you still get paid the same base pay. Even if you get a quarterly or yearly bonus, your family is affected daily by your decision to work more hours. Never think you are too invaluable to be let go. You may think, "Look at how much they pay me. They need me." No, this is all the more reason to hire someone cheaper and start them off at base pay. Don't mistake your high salary for being indispensable.

Here are a few suggestions on finding time:

- Try leaving on time, or an hour earlier than you normally do.
- Do some work while waiting at the beauty shop or barber shop.
- Print out pages you need to work on so you don't have to bring your computer home.
- Travel a lot? Get things done on or between flights and instead of socializing all night, head back to your room early and work on your dream.
- Put the kids to bed an hour earlier or just explain to them that between this certain hour, not to disturb you unless necessary or talk it over with your spouse and let him/her know that you need an hour of uninterrupted alone time each night.
- Make a list before hand of things you need to do when you have time and keep the list in your purse, wallet, or phone so when the time does come, you don't have to think about what you should be doing.

Be creative. There are many ways to carve out little bits of time that add up and make big differences.

The Rich Get Richer And The Poor Get Poorer

Sometimes in our quest for change, we get lax, we don't perform our best or give our all and then we have a tendency to look at others and compare, complain, or justify by making excuses for our shortcomings. We'll say things like "The rich get richer and the poor get poorer." Have you ever heard this? Of course you have. Is this a valid statement? Yes, it is. We see this statement play out every day in our society. Is it fair? Hmmm. Let's take a look. But wait. Not only do the rich get richer and the poor get poorer, the poor get rich and the rich get poor. There are many variations and situations that cause this plight in life. So again is it fair? Well, let's revisit the 25th chapter of Matthew, verses 28-29 NIV, the last verses in The Parable of Talents. *"Take the talent from him and give it to the one who has the ten talents. For everyone who has will be given more, and he will have an abundance. Whoever does not have, even what he has will be taken from him."*

Recall that the man gave different amounts of his property to his servants according to their ability and the two servants who received the most, doubled their "talents" and the one who received just one talent, buried his, so it was taken away and given to the servant who had the most talents. So is life fair? Yes, it most certainly is. To those who are given much, much is required. A talent was worth more than a thousand dollars. So what would you do if someone gave you a thousand dollars? No, don't say that no one will ever do that. Really, what would you do? Would you open up that business that has been in your heart? You know the one that you have been saying for years that someday you will do it? Or will you blow it by wasting it on unnecessary things? If you utilize what God has already given you, He will bless you with more.

Saving Your Gifts

But wait, what about the talents and gifts that you are wasting right now? You say you are saving them but just like the lazy servant, you are really wasting them. Consider the Bible passage. The servant did not make use of his talent. The text does not say the servant was jealous but allow me to use my imagination as to why he did not utilize his talent. Think about this--He received the least amount of money and was expected to do something with it. He also commented about the master getting the benefits without performing the labor. (I'm paraphrasing). So he may have been jealous of his master or the other two workers who received more than he. The servant may not have felt like he was receiving enough benefits which may have left him bitter and unwilling to make an extra effort.

We may be tempted to do the same thing in our vocations or places of employment. Some of us feel like we are underpaid and overworked already, and faced with the opportunity to take on another challenge or assignment, we are reluctant to, just as the servant was. However, the servants who doubled their master's money, were themselves blessed as well. These servants were not disgruntled at their master for giving them another assignment and expecting them to increase *his* investment. They were on the contrary, grateful and excited about the opportunity. The master did not disappoint them but rewarded them by enlarging their territory, their responsibility and their influence, and they also shared in his happiness. Just like the servants who increased their master's money, when we add value to others, to our employers, constituents, etc we enlarge our own territory and share in the success that we cause for others.

Many people want to wait until they get the title or position they want before they contribute their gifts and talents. Some of us are too concerned about the recognition we may pass up helping someone else. Others of us are jealous of the fact that we didn't get the assignment so we make sure we will not do any work to make it a success. In fact, some wish the project would fail just so they can justify they should have been the choice in the first place.

But your talents are never wasted. Even though you may be helping someone else, you are always learning from every experience. Even if you get no accolades, you have learned something that will help you fulfill your dream. I heard somewhere that you will have to help someone accomplish their dream before yours will be fulfilled. Be faithful with your gifts and talents, you will be noticed.

Even if not at your current employer, current team, or in your current position, your gifts and talents are being sharpened each time you put them to use. You should do your best with your talents even if you can not immediately see the benefit of using them because gifts and talents that are not used are lost. Give your best even if it's not your assignment. Give your best even if you're not working at the company you'd like to or on the team you feel you should be on. Continue to honor God in whatever you do. He will reward you.

And let us not be weary in well doing: for in due season we shall reap, if we faint not. Galatians 6:9 KJV

Remember the story of Joseph. Joseph was sold into slavery by his brothers. He worked very hard as a slave for his master Potiphar and God was pleased with Joseph.

As it turned out, God was with Joseph and things went very well with him. He ended up living in the home of his Egyptian master. His master recognized that God was with him, saw that God was working for good in everything he did. He became very fond of Joseph and made him his personal aide. He put him in charge of all his personal affairs, turning everything over to him. From that moment on, God blessed the home of the Egyptian—all because of Joseph. The blessing of God spread over everything he owned, at home and in the fields, and all Potiphar had to concern himself with was eating three meals a day. Genesis 39:2-6 The Message

Joseph could have been bitter because he was in slavery. He could have done the bare minimum to get by but he had a different, peculiar if you will, attitude. He worked as hard for his master as he would for himself. Joseph worked unto the Lord. He was so good in fact that his master had no concern, he did his work so thorough that there was no work for the master to do. Wow! In contrast, some employees are getting paid to do a job that they took the initiative to obtain but are doing the bare minimum to get by. They come late, leave early, and take more breaks than allowed. Some spend more time doing personal business on the company's time than the business the company is actually paying them to do.

I encourage you to be a good steward at work. Use your gifts and serve your company well, as unto God, and He will take care of you. It doesn't matter if your company changes, your group changes, or your manager. As long as God has favored you, you will not be harmed. Some of you work under almost unbearable circumstances and have every right to find something new. Some of you are putting up with some evil situations, maybe even witnessed some illegal practices but you still feel God has you there for a reason. Be encouraged, a man named Jacob was also in a drastic situation, yet he came out the victor. Listen to his work conditions.

…I see your father's countenance, that it is not toward me as before; but the God of my father hath been with me. And ye know that with all my power I have served your father. And your father hath deceived me, and changed my wages ten times; but God suffered him not to hurt me. Genesis 31:5-7 KJV

Now there's some things we'll put up with, but when you start messing with the money…! Some of the companies you work for are only prospering because you are employed there. God knows. Whether you decide to leave or stay at that particular place of employment, honor God in your behavior, speech, and attitude.

Work willingly at whatever you do, as though you were working for the Lord rather than for people. Colossians 3:23 New Living Translation

The Transition

While you are preparing for your next role or starting your own business, be careful who you share your dreams with. Joseph shared his dream with the ones closest to him, his brothers, and they in turn sold him into slavery. Even family members can get jealous of your dream and plot against you. Some people will take whatever information you give them and try to sabotage your endeavors. Be wise about the information you share, how much, and when you share it, since timing is important. You're not being secretive but selective.

A prudent man concealeth knowledge. Proverbs 12:23a KJV

Even friends can talk you out of your dream and plant seeds of doubt and insecurity if you let them. They may not even realize it, but some do. Don't let other people's hang-ups and insecurities hinder you. Don't let their limitations become your own. God gave *you* the vision so act on it.

Funding Your Dream

In the small business world it is said that if you're out of money, you're out of business. Be mindful that you need consistent inflow of money in order to make the business work. You can use the money you get from bonuses and raises on your current job to fund your dream. Open up a separate business account and start automatic deposits into it from your checking account. You also need to do all you can to minimize your overhead. Think twice before you make purchases, especially if what you are buying will not generate income. If you need office furniture, buy used instead of new. Explore ways to split advertising costs with another company. Use electronic communication to decrease supply costs. Try bartering instead of paying for products and services. Bartering is exchanging goods or services that you provide for goods or services that you need, and does not involve money. For instance, if you are starting a carpet-cleaning business and you need marketing services performed, you could offer to clean the carpets in the person's home that you need the marketing services from rather than paying money for it.

Protecting Your Dream

As you fund your dream you also need to guard it. You may have intellectual property that needs protecting; get the copyright, trademark, or patent you need. Research the credentials, licenses, registrations you need, etc. Also, be careful not to be taken advantage of. People feel like Christians are trusting and therefore easy prey so they will disguise *themselves* as Christians to get closer to an unsuspecting Christian. Some customers will try to take advantage of you by short paying or not paying at all. To avoid this, I suggest you require a 50% up-front fee before you do any work and make sure the customer pays for all the materials.

Use this same concept when providing any type of service. It's hard to tell the difference between Christians and just church folk so keep the same policy with everyone. Just because someone says they are a Christian doesn't make them one.

You Have Arrived

Congratulations! So you have arrived. Let me talk specifically to those who are monetarily rich for a moment. I specify monetarily rich because when you say someone is rich, people automatically assume you're talking in monetary terms. You can be rich in many different areas. You can also be rich in one area and poor in another. You can be financially rich but emotionally poor, financially rich but can't enjoy it because you have poor relationships. There are millionaires who can't sleep at night because they don't trust the person they're sleeping with or they constantly have others pulling them from every direction, trying to get a piece of their pie.

To the financially rich I say this; it is not your responsibility to take care of your extended family, your friends, etc. Sure it's nice to help out so if you can afford to pay off your sister's house just as easy as you could buy a happy meal, then be a blessing to your sister and your extended family. However, know your limits regarding what you can and cannot do when it comes to helping. There are countless stories of celebrities, entertainers, athletes, and lottery winners who have gone from riches to rags. They have "had it all" and "lost it all" possibly because some act like God and try to supply everybody's needs. You do not have an unlimited supply, but God does. You can't please everyone. That's a burden that is not yours to bear. There's also a difference in being a blessing and being a crutch.

I've heard it said that money doesn't change you, it changes the people around you. You will have some family members and friends who feel entitled to your money; go figure. They can even make you feel guilty for having so much money but you should not give out of guilt and remember that you are not a bank. You are the one who made the sacrifices to get where you are today. You are the one who put in the time, effort, and risk. It was your name on the line. You are the one who got up early, and stayed late while others lived the status quo. Do not feel obligated to give to others what your blood, sweat, and tears have paid for. You can give all of your money away and a number of people still won't be satisfied.

In fact some people, even those closest to you, would be more satisfied if you lost all your money and came back down to their level financially. It's sad to say but some Christians still have the crabs-in-a-bucket mentality, they see you about to climb up out of the bucket to freedom and will grab hold of you to pull you back down so you can all die together. (Go crabbing and see this in action.) If all of your money is gone, what then? Do you really think you can call those same family members, friends, and associates who had their hands in your pockets, to give *you* some money? Probably not.

Now the reality is that not everyone is after your money so don't change just because you have a lot of it. Don't disassociate yourself from those you love because you have a few more dollars right now, be an inspiration to them. Give inspiration to the young adults who watched you get where you are and to the little kids who want to be like you. Be grateful for those who prayed for you, to those who helped your parents care for you, and to those who did things for you that you know nothing about. Remember the teacher or coach who took out the extra time and effort to see you succeed. Remember the uncle or aunt who helped out and stood in the gap for an absent parent. (A parent can live in the home and still be absent.) There are many instances where people have made tremendous sacrifices to help a child succeed, regardless if the child was theirs or not, only to be forgotten when the child turns adult and now has it all together. Sure you can say it was their job and you don't owe them anything but no man succeeds completely independent of any human being. Do give back.

As you are preserving your money, always remember who provided and continues to provide the wealth. No; not the baseball owner, the agent, promoter, or yourself, but God and God alone.

You may say to yourself, "My power and the strength of my hands have produced this wealth for me." But remember the Lord your God, for it is he who gives you the ability to produce wealth...Deuteronomy 8:17-18 NIV

Be mindful to give credit where credit is due. Don't give credit to luck, coincidence, or even to you. Always remember your source. Do not be foolish in thinking that you have done this on your own. Even though you put in the time and practice, God allowed you to have the talent, the health, the physical attributes needed, and the mind to think the necessary thoughts. He allowed you to be in the right place at the right time. He allowed that scout to see your potential, He allowed you to get that medical scholarship, the residency, the needed vote, etc. Everything and anything you needed came from Him alone. When you recognize who the ultimate thanks should go to, you will give back with an attitude of gratitude.

Now that you have "arrived" and have everything and anything you need financially, we'll look at ways to keep your wealth in the savings chapter.

Things to Remember

- Pregnant with possibility
- *Good Times*
- Scale of Positivity
- Good Seeds
- Parable of the Talents
- Joseph

More Living Your Dreams Scriptures

But they that wait upon the LORD shall renew their strength; they shall mount up with wings as eagles; they shall run, and not be weary; and they shall walk, and not faint. Isaiah 40:31 KJV

He that is faithful in that which is least is faithful also in much: and he that is unjust in the least is unjust also in much. If therefore ye have not been faithful in the unrighteous mammon, who will commit to your trust the true riches? And if ye have not been faithful in that which is another man's, who shall give you that which is your own? Luke 16:10-12 KJV

Moreover it is required in stewards, that a man be found faithful. I Corinthians 4:2 KJV

For the love of money is the root of all evil: which while some coveted after, they have erred from the faith, and pierced themselves through with many sorrows. I Timothy 6:10 KJV

Every man also to whom God hath given riches and wealth, and hath given him power to eat thereof, and to take

his portion, and to rejoice in his labour; this is the gift of God. Ecclesiastes 5:19 KJV

The slothful man roasteth not that which he took in hunting: but the substance of a diligent man is precious. Proverbs 12:27 KJV

Whoever loves money never has money enough; whoever loves wealth is never satisfied with his income. Ecclesiastes 5:10 NIV

A faithful man shall abound with blessings: but he that maketh haste to be rich shall not be innocent. Proverbs 28:20 KJV

But mark this: There will be terrible times in the last days. People will be lovers of themselves, lovers of money, boastful, proud, abusive, disobedient to their parents, ungrateful, unholy, without love, unforgiving, slanderous, without self-control, brutal, not lovers of the good, treacherous, rash, conceited, lovers of pleasure rather than lovers of God--having a form of godliness but denying its power. Have nothing to do with them. 2 Tim 3:1-5 NIV

This is the only life you will have so plan it well.
—**Shalonda McFarland**

Chapter Five
Planning

The Eye of the Bull

Where there is no vision, the people perish: but he that keepeth the law, happy is he.
Proverbs 29:18 KJV

Commit to the Lord whatever you do and your plans will succeed.
Proverbs 16:3 NIV

Planning is the key. Some people get their lives situated and established, they get their career, house, money in the bank, and then they start a family. Some do this simultaneously, and others in reverse order. There is no one "right" way to plan your life, for there are many paths that lead to success. Those paths may intermingle, you may have unexpected twists and turns, or unseen dips or gravel along your way but at least take the necessary steps to prepare for the journey so you reach your desired destination. This is your life. Think about where you want to go and how you will get there.

Sadly, what many people do is just let things happen with little or no planning. They live in the moment and assume things will just work out because they are a child of God, but His word says we must have a vision. A vision is simply a plan. Some of us take more time planning a wedding than we do our marriage, and planning a party than our life. We make decisions before we consider the outcome and never question if the timing is right. For instance, we start having babies before we consider the cost needed to care for them, financially and otherwise. This can put a lot of financial strain on a marriage if you don't plan this and other major life-changing events before they happen. Not estimating the cost causes one to have their car repossessed and their home foreclosed on. The old adage still applies today-If you fail to plan, you plan to fail.

Suppose one of you wants to build a tower. Will he not first sit down and estimate the cost to see if he has enough money to complete it? For if he lays the foundation and is not able to finish it, everyone who sees it will ridicule him, saying, "This fellow began to build and was not able to finish." Luke 14:28-29 NIV

S.M.A.R.T. Goals

Planning involves setting goals and in order to have effective goals, I want to share with you a concept I learned at one of my employers. In order to see your goals accomplished you need to make sure your goals are SMART—Specific, Measureable, Attainable, Relevant, and Time-bound. Let me explain and give examples of each.

- **Specific**-Being as precise as you can. Instead of saying I want to lose weight, you would say I want to lose 15 lbs of body fat.
- **Measureable**-The progress of the goal can be tracked and you clearly know when you have reached the goal; therefore there's no ambiguity. You can weigh yourself before and during

your quest to lose weight therefore the loss of 15 pounds can be measured.
- **Attainable**-When the goal is realistic, it can be achieved. Losing 15 pounds of body fat in two days is not a realistic goal.
- **Relevant**-The goal has meaning or a purpose for you. It is *your* goal and it will help you achieve higher goals. Your goal of losing 15 pounds may be so you can drop a dress size or have a toned, healthier body.
- **Time-bound**-There is a timeframe in which to achieve the goal. The timeframe should be realistic yet challenging. Losing 15 pounds of body fat within 5 years is realistic but may not be challenging.

Even when you have SMART goals, you need to write them down. You are much more likely to attain your goals when they are on paper. An unwritten goal is only a wish.

And the LORD answered me, and said, Write the vision, and make it plain upon tables, that he may run that readeth it. Habakkuk 2:2 KJV

Your Vision

Along with writing out your goals, or capturing your vision on paper, you need a plan of action. This will keep you focused on what steps you need to take to achieve your goal. You know how teachers tell you in school to make a to-do list? You write down everything you need to accomplish that day and arrange the list according to priority. You list the important things first and second most important thing second, and so forth.

Well, regarding making your vision or financial to-do list, formulating a monthly spending plan needs to be at the top of your list. This is the number one item on your to-do list. What is a spending plan or what some would call a cash flow plan? O.K. Here it is-brace yourself, a b-u-d-g-e-t, yes a budget. I know you expected rocket science. Sorry to disappoint you with such a simple and common concept. A budget is simply a written plan for your money, a guide, a cash flow plan. A cash flow plan is something I'm sure you've heard of before, but probably have not put it into practice. Somehow, the word budget has a negative connotation associated with it. Immediately when I said that word you may have had feelings like: I'm not going to be able to buy the things I want; that's too much work; those just do not work; I'm doing fine, I have more money than some, so I don't need a budget, etc.

In response to those thoughts, let me just say, I've thought all of them too and whether you are single or married you do need a budget. If you're single, you alone control your budget, which can be good or bad based on your personality. Some people need an accountability partner to help them stay on track or just a sounding board when facing decisions. This needed accountability is almost automatic in a marriage, but if you are single you could seek out an accountability partner in the form of an advisor or counselor, even if this could be a challenge because you are intimidated about talking to someone. If you have the desire to be married, you have the opportunity during your season of singleness, to get your money right before other variables are added to your life.

If you're married, you may have had other choice thoughts about budgeting depending on your perspective of whether you're the saver or the spender in your marriage. Most marriages typically have one spender and one saver, which summarizes your natural tendency regarding money. It's highly unlikely that both spouses have the same mindset about money. I believe this is God's way of balancing things but if a couple doesn't communicate, it can lead to tension and frustration. I also think this is evidence that God has a great sense of humor. (Well, marriage itself is evidence of that.)

If you have two spenders they're probably out of control financially, with little to no savings, and heavily in debt. If you have two savers, they probably have a lot of money stored, but have no life. In my marriage, I am the saver, my husband is the spender. Without me, my husband would be broke, (sorry Dear) and without him I'd have no life. I would just save, and save, and save without enjoying the fruits of my labor. And without me, my husband wouldn't have anything for retirement because he would be spending money like mad, with no clear plan. I did not understand me and my husband's differences in this area at first; I thought he was a frivolous spender and he thought I was a tightwad. After all these years of marriage we still have this basic view of each other's tendencies, but we have learned to value the other's overall views and to compromise. We've both become better people with money matters. Just like iron sharpens iron, we complement each other. He's become a better saver, and I've learned to live a little.

Back to budgeting; let me share a story with you. Hopefully by hearing this, you'll have a new perspective on proactively planning how you spend your money every month, *before* the month begins. I do not even remember where I heard this story but it stuck with me as I hope it will with you. Here it goes...

The Eye Of The Bull

A reporter was passing through a small town and noticed the most perfect marksmanship he had ever seen. He saw trees where a highly talented marksman had shot his arrow dead center of the bulls-eye target. Each tree he saw was a perfect shot. After seeing the first arrow in the bulls-eye, the reporter thought, "How lucky." As he continued walking through the town, he saw a second arrow through the bulls-eye, then a third, and as he lifted his head and looked across the pond to where the forest began, amazingly he saw what seemed like a hundred trees that had perfectly-shot arrows in the middle of each and every target. This reporter had never seen such accuracy and precision. How could this be? He had to meet such a person. What a talent, what a gift! How many hours of practice, dedication, and complete devotion one must commit to have such excellence in this sport? Is this person an Olympian? How he wanted to meet this highly dedicated person! With eagerness he hurried over to the town hall to seek where he could find this person. Being a reporter, he was already drafting in his mind how his column would read, "Excellence in the small town of..." He finally reached the town hall and asked one of the citizens where he could find this excellent marksman. The citizen matter-of-factly told him, "Oh that's just the town blacksmith. Yes, he shot those arrows alright. But he shoots them in the trees first and then he goes back and draws in the target. That way he never misses."

So the moral of the story—Don't go through your financial life just shooting arrows and then drawing the target after the fact. That's exactly what you do when you do not have a plan. When you do not have a budget you are just like that man who never wants to miss, who never wants to take inventory of where his strengths and opportunities are, who is afraid of missing the mark, who does not want to apply himself or make improvements. He has no sense of accomplishment. He is living life in what he thinks is the safe zone but he is really just going through the motions with nothing to show for it.

When you do not budget, and you find yourself at the end of the month, what have you accomplished? Where did your money go? Money will do whatever you tell it to do, whatever you plan it to do. I used to look at my checkbook and wonder where all the money went. I was making good money but I was still in debt even though I had a 401k, stocks, and assets, I wasn't where I wanted or needed to be financially. Furthermore, it is hard to have peace of mind when you owe money.

Need more convincing on budgeting? Just think of how a company conducts business. Think about the company you work for. Every company has a plan. Most small businesses plan at least five years in advance. Most corporations must plan ten to twenty years ahead. They look at their overall strategy and how it lines up with the company's mission or vision statement. Companies look at the long and short term and they plan down to every last detail.

Those of you who own stocks in a company get a quarterly prospectus on the company. It has the detail of income, outflow, assets and liabilities, etc. You expect this detail in a company because some answer to Wall Street and stockholders, correct? Why not expect the same in your company, your howbeit, small company of three to six people, called a family? What are your long and short-term goals? Do they line up with your vision? Do you have regular board meetings with your spouse to gain alignment or to rethink a strategy that both of you have agreed on? Do you look at *your* prospectus, your net worth? Like a corporation, do you plan how your money is spent each month via a cash flow plan or a budget? Why not start now?

Do not say you will start next month. Do it now or you probably will not do it at all. Do not put it off. If you wait until next week, it will turn into two weeks, then three months…months add up to years…years roll on to retirement. If you do not change now, you will have the same thing to show for it 30 years from now. If you do not make any adjustments, what will your life be like and what will you have accomplished?

Look at it this way, if you make $30,000 a year and work for 30 years, you would have made $900,000. This example is just to keep it simple. Hopefully you'd get a raise along the way and earn at least twice as much a year at the 30-year mark. If you make $50,000, in 30 years you would have made $1,500,000, (one million five hundred thousand dollars!) These numbers get better if you're married and have two incomes.

These numbers tell me several things. First, we are all millionaires, even if it takes a lifetime. Second, we are held accountable for how we use the money that passes through our hands so stop making excuses and start now. Really, I mean put this book down at this very moment and draft out your budget. You owe it to yourself and to your family. You are the president and CEO of your corporation and you owe it to your stockholders and employees (your spouse and children) to plan and grow your company. Leave a legacy.

• • • •

Hopefully, I have convinced you to start a budget, and there are some available online. You should pick one that you are most comfortable with or create your own on a spreadsheet if that is more comfortable. I would first suggest that you look at some budgets that are already available to you, so you'll have a frame of reference. You want to make sure not to forget anything, so I highly advise you to check out what's out there before you reinvent the wheel.

Having a budget will help you stay on track with your financial goals, but there are many things that can get you off track if you let them. Let's examine a few. The following can be some of the biggest budget busters. If not planned, these can really set you back financially—buying a house or car, having children, vacations, Christmas, and losing a job.

Buying A House

Many people in the financial industry will tell you that owning a house is your greatest asset. They say this because of the tax advantages owning a home brings, and the assumption that your home's value will increase and be worth much more than the price you paid for it. Yet, if you stop making monthly payments, you'll see that a house is a liability, not an asset. Owning your own home is a worthy dream that many of us seek, but if we acquire it too soon or on the wrong terms, it can be an extreme financial burden. Even if you buy too much house at a steal, you may not be able to afford the upkeep a bigger house requires. There is more to owning a home than meets the eye. Before you jump from renting to owning, make sure you consider all the costs. The grass may be greener on the other side, but it costs more to keep it that way. Consider these financial costs of owning a traditional home vs. renting an apartment:

- Down payment--The mortgage company will typically require you to give 20% of the loan amount as a down payment. For a $140,000 home that is $28,000.
- PMI Insurance--If you can not afford this down payment, you will be required to get insurance which is around $150 a month or the mortgage company will make a second loan out of the 20%, $28,000 in this scenario, and assign it a higher interest rate.
- Monthly note plus taxes (school, MUD, and property)--The monthly note on a home includes more than just the note, but taxes as well. Some homeowners will pay their taxes each month along with their mortgage payment and the mortgage company will set the taxes aside in an Escrow Account to accumulate with each monthly payment until the required amount of money is available to pay the taxes at the end of each year. A typical yearly amount is a combined $3,100 or $258 a month. If you elect not to have an escrow account, you must be disciplined enough to save up this money on your own so you'll have it in January, when yearly taxes are due.
- Utility bills will typically be higher. Homes are naturally bigger than apartments, and the big-

ger space requires more money to light, keep cool, and heat.
- Water bill--Some apartments don't require you to pay this, so this would be an extra expense, around $50 to $150 a month.
- Insurance (structural, loss of use, and flood)--Insurance on a home is mandatory. The mortgage company requires you to have insurance, unlike an apartment where the management says you need renter's insurance but does not enforce it. A typical yearly policy can range from $1,500 on up depending on various factors. Flood insurance is not mandatory and also varies in price, around $300 a year.
- Maintenance--In a typical apartment, there are no maintenance costs unlike a home where you must do everything yourself or hire someone to do it. Either way, you will pay for the costs. A home requires mowing the lawn each week or every two weeks. This takes money and time. A lawnmower and all the tools associated for keeping a nice lawn can easily run you $500, or a typical fee to have it mowed is $30 each time ($780 a year if you have it done every other week). To self mow you may need not only the lawn mower but a weed eater, rake, water hose, shovel, blower, outdoor broom, gas for mower, etc.
- Home Association Fees--Due yearly, typically in January, these fees can range from $300-$600 or higher, depending on your neighborhood.
- Buying Appliances--Most homes will have the stove and dishwasher already in the price of the house, but some homes do not come with a washer ($300) and dryer ($250) or refrigera-

tor ($1,200).
- Household Repairs--Homeowners are responsible for all repairs versus calling the maintenance man in an apartment. This includes everything from a leaky roof to a clogged sink.
- Mortgage interest--If you have a mortgage on your home, there are interest charges to consider. How much can interest charges effect the cost of a home? For example, if you buy a house that cost $113,540 on a 30-year loan at a 6.375% interest rate, at the end of the term, due to the interest charges, one would end up paying $255,004. In this example you waste over $141,000 in interest alone. That is a lot of money!

Yes, there are of course many benefits to owning a home, one being the tax advantage. Yes, there are tax advantages to owning versus renting but they do not outweigh the interest you pay to the bank every month for the mortgage note. To avoid paying interest, the ideal situation, although some would say not realistic for them, would be to buy a new or drastically reduced used or foreclosure home with cash. This is rarely done however, because not too many people have the discipline to save up over $100,000 over multiple years, therefore they usually get a 15 to 30-year mortgage.

Buying A Car

Like buying a house, it's better to buy a car with cash and avoid the interest rather than financing it. Although with a house, it's better to rent until you can afford to buy, with a car it's better to buy than to rent, or lease as they say in the car business. I won't go into details on the many negatives about leasing but I will talk about things you should consider when buying a vehicle.

- Before you buy a car, consider renting the car you want to buy, like you would if you were on vacation, to see if you indeed want that one. Look at the functionality, storage space, safety ratings, leg room for you and your passengers, etc. Do some research on the internet to see its resale value. What is the market value and trade value of the vehicle? If I had to guess, the average amount of time we spend on the car lot is 5 hours yet we spend limited time doing research on a vehicle that if financed may take us 5 ½ years to pay off. Once the new car smell wears off, which takes a few weeks, you are left with a big liability and a $400 a month car note for the next 60+ months.
- It's better to buy pre-owned or used rather than new since cars depreciate as soon as you drive off the car lot.
- The newer your car is the more it costs to insure and the higher the registration fees.
- The more gadgets and gismos you put on your vehicle, like rims, sound systems, and t.v.'s, the more it cost to insure (and the more likely it is to be stolen).
- If you do finance the car, wait until you have totally paid off the car before you pay the tax title and license, otherwise it gets lumped into the loan amount, and you will pay the interest rate on that too.
- Get G.A.P. insurance, which pays your car off if it gets totaled and you owe more on the car than what it's worth. Without it, the insurance

company will only pay the cars value, but if you owe more money on it than its value, there's a gap between what the insurance will cover and what you have left to pay. Essentially you could be paying a car note on a car that is no longer usable if you don't have GAP insurance. Remember to ask for a prorated refund of your GAP insurance if you pay your car off early.

Having Children

Children are a tremendous blessing to any parent. Your life changes forever as soon as they are conceived, not just when they are born. Since they do change your life forever, when making the decision to have a baby, make sure you consider all the costs involved so that you are blessed, not stressed, with your little bundle of joy. Kids can be very expensive! Please don't be naïve about that. And as a parent, you are totally responsible for them legally, until they turn age 18, financially—who knows, since there are a lot of grown children still living and depending on their parents. Whether legally, financially, morally, or spiritually, parenting is a never-ending job. Ideally a baby is born into a marriage between two loving people, husband and wife, but today, there are many different circumstances in which children are born. There are single mothers, single fathers, divorced fathers, grandparents raising their grandchildren, and teen mothers. There are many teen parents that have not broken the poverty cycle because they have children that they can't afford to provide for.

Even in a marriage you can get overwhelmed with the costs of having one or more children. I am not saying you need to plan all the surprise out of having kids and I don't want the costs of having and caring for children deter you from having them. I just want you to be aware of the costs and be better prepared for when the time is right. You should make preparation for children mentally and financially and you should also discuss your expectations with your spouse way before the baby arrives. The following are a few things to consider when making the decision to have children:

- Will the baby go to daycare?
- How much does daycare cost a month?
- What are the differences in costs between daycares that are where I work versus where I live?
- What are the daycare hours and how does that correspond with my job's hours?
- What happens when one or both of us has to go to work early, before the daycare opens? Or work late after the day care closes?
- Who will take and pick up the baby from daycare? Which days?
- Who will take off from work when the baby gets sick? (Trust me, they will get sick.)
- How much does formula cost? How often do we need to buy it?
- And diapers? Baby food? Clothes? Bottles? Shots? Health insurance? Baby bed? Stroller? Car seat? Swing? High chair?
- How much will these costs add to our monthly budget?
- Does my job offer a dependent care reserve account?
- What will the insurance deductible be for the delivery?

That's just the first year! So are you ready? If not, at least you know you're not ready and are better prepared to get ready. I hope I did not discourage you but armed you with knowledge. Children truly are gifts from God.

Sons are a heritage from the Lord, children a reward from him. Like arrows in the hands of a warrior are sons born in one's youth. Blessed is the man whose quiver is full of them. Psalms 127:3-5 NIV

Vacation or Staycation

A house and a car are semi-permanent things we buy that can break our budgets, and children are definitely permanent, but vacations are temporary yet they have the same budget-busting power if not planned correctly.

As we approach the end of each school year, the summer months signal another season of travel. The question that likely arises is, "Where are we going on vacation?" But the more important question is, "Can we afford a vacation?" If you can not afford a vacation or just do not want to travel, an alternative to a vacation is a staycation. A staycation is a vacation you take right at home, in your area. A staycation is cheaper, just as fun, and can be more relaxing than vacationing in another city or state.

A staycation can involve a tour of your city or immediate suburb. You'd be amazed at how much you can find to see and do, right in your own "backyard." You'd be surprised at how much you overlook activities and places of interest that are all around you. Google or Bing your town and you will discover a variety of sites to visit and a lot of things to do. It is ironic how many people visit the cities and towns we live in to see the sites we aren't even aware of while we travel to their cities to see what they've never experienced.

Vacations can be expensive. So can you afford one? If you answer "NO" to any of these questions you may not be able to:

- Do I have money saved for an emergency?
- Can I pay for this vacation in full?
- Are my bills caught up?

Simple questions but you'd be surprised how many people take a vacation without considering these. You do not want to put yourself in a financial bind over a few days of fun. And do not let these excuses cause you to make an unwise decision to take a vacation you can't afford:

- I deserve it.
- The kids deserve it.
- We normally go every year, I do not want to ruin things by not going this year.
- Everything is cheaper, I just can't miss these deals.

If you are still paying off a vacation after you've returned home, the regrets over the bills will outweigh the memories. Some of us take vacation every year but still live paycheck to paycheck. We'd be better off saving the money we would spend on vacation for everyday living expenses. Keep in mind the total cost of a vacation:

- Hotel-room rate plus state and local taxes
- Airfare-tickets plus taxes and baggage fees
- Rental car-rate plus taxes and gas
- Gas or airport parking fees if you fly
- Amusement park-tickets plus taxes, parking, souvenirs, and food
- Food-three meals a day plus gratuity taxes and snacks
- Misc.-camera film, film processing, clothes (you'll realize you or your children can not fit last year's shorts as you're packing the suitcases)

There is nothing wrong with vacations, they are fun and relaxing. The problem lies when we spend too much money and over tax ourselves in order to take them. Consider downsizing your vacation so that when you return, you will still enjoy your life. Vacation or staycation, that is the question!

Christmas

Not as expensive as a car, but maybe as expensive as a vacation, spending money on Christmas gifts can also bust the budget and the bank account. If you are not careful, you will get caught up in the buying frenzy and spend more money than you ever intended. Spending thousands of dollars on gifts is not unheard of. Even if you just spend hundreds of dollars, if you can't afford it, don't do it. Don't let your emotions take over and cause you to make a poor decision. You shouldn't still be paying on Christmas the following March. Unfortunately this does happen because it is very easy to go over your budget. Christians are naturally givers because we are followers of Christ. God is the giver of all things good and Jesus Christ gave the ultimate gift of His life for us. So as we imitate Christ we are naturally generous but sometimes our strengths, if unbalanced, can be our weakness. You more than likely can't afford to buy everyone a gift. You might not even be able to afford to buy gifts for your immediate family. So what. Christmas is not about buying gifts. It's Jesus' birthday. Give Him a gift by serving others. If you do want to buy gifts for others, here are a few suggestions to make your money stretch each Christmas:

- Buy gifts year round-There are always sales out there. Keep a look out on good bargains when you see them. Even when you may not be sure who the gift should go to, if you know it's a nice gift, get it. You'll find someone to give it to later.
- Make your gift-Put together a scrapbook or buy an inexpensive photo album and fill it up with photos, or take a family photo with your digital camera, print it out, frame it, and gift-wrap it.
- Bake your gift-Bake cookies, brownies, or fudge and put it in a nice container that you buy from the local dollar store.
- Write a letter-Write a heart-felt, sincere letter to someone. Thank them for who they are, and what they mean to you, what they've done in the past, present, and the good thoughts you have for them in the future. You can give them to your spouse, parent, sibling, friend, pastor, or use as an encouraging letter to a struggling teen in your church or one of your students at school.

Black Friday

In addition to non-traditional gifts and buying gifts year round, many of us are going to wait for that special day when the discounts are huge and everywhere. That day is Black Friday. Don't be ashamed if you participate and look forward to this yearly buying opportunity. Everyone wants to get the best deals and make their money stretch so take advantage of this special day.

Black Friday is always the day after Thanksgiving. Thanksgiving always falling on a Thursday, and the following day a Friday, is normally the first time all year that retailers see their money go from red (losing money) to black (making money), hence the name Black Friday. The stores put out these amazing ads and the public goes crazy; some of us will be at the store at 4 a.m. to get that deal. You want to get the most out of the retailers' price war without going overboard on your spending, which is very easy to do. Well, to make the most of Black Friday here are a few suggestions and things to look out for.

To avoid overspending, think about your purchase, for example, just because that flat-screen T.V. is 80% off, it still may cost over $1000. You should make your decision to buy based on if you can afford the retail price, not because you just can't pass up a T.V. that's so drastically marked down. Remember you still have to eat the next day and your bills will still come in the same time the next month. For those of us with children, consider that your baby will more than likely play with the box than the expensive toy that came in the box. The more toys you buy for your small toddler, the more toys you'll have to pick up off of the floor months down the line. The more games, gadgets, and gizmos you buy for your teenager, the more they want. There's always something else to buy. My children, with all the stuff they possess, have told me on more than one occasion that they are bored. So don't stress yourself in thinking you need to get them more this year. More does not mean better. Give something from the heart and be at peace.

Do:

- Know how much you are willing to spend for all presents combined.
- Have your list prepared before you shop.
- Pay in cash–This will make you less likely to overspend because it hurts to physically see all those dollar bills leaving your hand and going to the clerk. (If you'd have to carry a lot of money, use a debit card instead, to be safe.)
- Circle the items you want to buy from each Ad-This will keep you focused and will give you time to think about each item before you get into the store.

Don't:

- Spend more than you budgeted
- Get a loan for Christmas
- Use credit cards
- Feel guilty, splurge, or lose your head

Save Time/Avoid the Crowd:

- Go two days before, pick out what you want in department stores and have it held for 48 hrs.

Then you can just go to the cashier and pick it up without having to look through what's been picked over or stand in line for the fitting room.
- Buy gift cards; just make sure the person actually shops there.
- Buy the gift you know you want a week or two before Black Friday. Some stores will give you your money back for the difference in price if what you bought goes down in price within 30 days of your purchase. Just make sure to keep your receipt and the Ad.
- Shop on the internet, you may find the same deal with free shipping. Also, some retailers have their Black Friday prices on the internet for the entire week.
- Cyber Monday-The Monday following Black Friday is when many retailers will have special online deals just for those shopping on the internet.

Losing A Job

Okay, back to a more serious subject. Losing a job can be catastrophic, especially if you are already living paycheck to paycheck. One thing this current economy has taught us is that no one is exempt from a layoff. You can be an ideal employee and still be laid off. You can have a Master's or PhD and still be out of a job. People get laid off in bad times and good times, days before Christmas, six months after being promoted and moving yourself to an unknown city, before a merger, after an acquisition, because of department downsizing due to low sales, and whether you've been with a company for twenty years or two. It matters not whether you are the janitor or the junior partner;

you can't always predict who, when, or why when it comes to change. These things are not in your control. What is in your control, is how prepared you are if the time comes. Do you have a safety net in case of an emergency? Do you have an umbrella for the rain? Do you have a fire extinguisher in case of a fire? Your fire extinguisher is an emergency fund. Just like the fire extinguisher sits in the corner as the sign on the glass says, "Break In Case of Emergency," you need money set aside that you know you can go to in case of a financial emergency. The question you need to answer is, "If I lose my job today, how long can I go without a paycheck?" What if it's two to six weeks?

You should always have money set aside in an emergency fund, or rainy day fund for financial emergencies. It doesn't matter what you call it, just as long as you have it when you need it. How much money is enough? Well, how charged would you keep a fire extinguisher? You never know how big the fire is going to be so you keep it fully charged. What does that mean? It's really a matter of how secure you feel with what level of money you have saved. You figure that amount based on how much your monthly expenses are. Some people have one month of expenses saved, some three, some six, some twelve. Some people may not feel secure with just six months, while others may feel really secure with three months worth. Other factors to consider when deciding on how much money to keep in a rainy day fund are:

- How many months will it rain? (How many months will I be out of a job?)
- Are you single or married? Do you have a family that depends on your income?
- If you're single, could you temporarily move

back home with your parents if necessary? (See, I told you parenting never stops.)
- Do you have a niche skill set or are you in an executive level position which may take longer to find?
- Are you making twice as much money doing a job because of your length of service at a particular company that is not congruent to what you see in the marketplace?

These are only a few examples to consider when deciding how much money one should put in an emergency fund. The point is, the time to plan for an emergency is before it happens, not during. Just like you wouldn't wait for a fire to plan the escape route but you'd have multiple routes mapped out in advance.

We've talked about SMART goals, budgeting, purchasing large semi-permanent items and small temporary ones. We've even discussed planning for life events such as children and changes in job status. There are many situations in life and just as many paths one may take. Whatever chapter you are presently writing in your book of life, plan that and subsequent chapters well.

Things To Remember

- SMART Goals
- Bull's Eye
- Umbrella
- Fire Extinguisher
- Escape Routes

More Planning Scriptures

May he give you the desire of your heart and make all your plans succeed. Psalms 20:4 NIV

Plans are established by seeking advice. Proverbs 20:18a NIV

But the noble make noble plans, and by noble deeds they stand. Isaiah 32:8 NIV

All hard work brings a profit, but mere talk leads only to poverty. Proverbs 14:23 NIV

The plans of the diligent lead to profit as surely as haste leads to poverty. Proverbs 21:5 NIV

Lazy hands make for poverty, but diligent hands bring wealth. Proverbs 10:4 NIV

Wealth is not determined by how much you make but by how much you keep.
—**Shalonda McFarland**

Chapter Six
Saving

Make the Buffalo Holler

You lazy fool, look at an ant. Watch it closely; let it teach you a thing or two. Nobody has to tell it what to do. All summer it stores up food; at harvest it stockpiles provisions. So how long are you going to laze around doing nothing? How long before you get out of bed? A nap here, a nap there, a day off here, a day off there, sit back, take it easy—do you know what comes next? Just this: You can look forward to a dirt-poor life, poverty your permanent houseguest!
Proverbs 6:6-11 The Message Bible

My grandma, Ms. Lorena Chaney has always told me that I hold on to a nickel so tight, you can hear the buffalo holler. This is another way of her saying I don't like to spend money. (For the young crowd--back in the day, the face of a nickel had a buffalo on it.) I am a saver by nature so it is very easy for me not to spend money. As we discussed earlier, most people tend to be either a saver or a spender. Even though you may be a spender by nature, you can still save. In fact it is wise to save.

Just like the ant has a natural instinct to store up food (save), God's children possess the spiritual wisdom and natural instinct to save, and be good stewards of the resources He has allowed us to have. You must save now in order to have anything worthwhile to spend later. Saving is a necessity and responsible thing we do to protect our way of life. In the last chapter I touched on why we save for a rainy day and keep our umbrella handy in case situations arise. Most people won't argue the fact that one must save for a rainy day yet there are many people who face sudden calamity and destruction because they do not save any money.

Many people live from paycheck to paycheck and never get ahead because they spend every red cent they make and then some. When they've exhausted their money, they go and find another source—they borrow. (We'll discuss that in the next chapter.) Saving is essential to your financial health. Your financial health also affects your emotional, social, and psychological health and is a reflection of your spiritual health.

Since saving is part of your financial health then why do many people have inadequate savings or no savings at all? Why don't more people save? I'll offer up a few reasons. Some people suffer from a common disease known as Stuffitice. Stuffitice is a condition that makes a person want more stuff. The more things they have the better they feel. This is also called materialism. Some people feel entitled to more things even when they clearly can't afford them and the more they buy, the less they have to save. Along with materialism, some are never satisfied. They are not content with what they have. When one is not content, you will constantly look for things to please you but with each purchase comes ultimate dissatisfaction. When a person is not content, it can simply be called ungrateful and greed is a close cousin to ungratefulness. Along with materialism, discontent, and ungratefulness is no self control, and habit. When adults lack self control we act just like children who want things now even when we lack the wisdom to know how to handle the very thing that we desire. This is a sign of a lack of maturity. Immaturity will cause you to buy something you want and then try to justify it as a need, even though you can't afford it. Immaturity will cause you to buy something now on credit, instead of placing something in layaway, saving up the money for the purchase, or doing without it altogether.

Like lack of self control, when you have a habit, you just don't care. You don't even think about what you're doing, you just keep on spending. You're on autopilot. This is similar to you driving home from work every day and on one particular day you don't even remember how you arrived home. Has this ever happened to you? You are so accustomed to driving the exact same route home that you don't even have to think about it. It's now easy to stop paying attention to what's going on because everything is so familiar. This is why most vehicular incidents occur close to home. Apply this same driving principle to your financial habits. Change your financial routine, the financial path you continue to take without even thinking about it.

Do you see yourself with any of these before-mentioned attitudes? Now that we've gone through reasons why some do not save, let's look at ways to save. It is true, we live in uncertain times. There are so many financial challenges people face these days. Companies are no longer loyal to employees, taxes on income and homes have skyrocketed as has the cost of living, and incomes have not increased at the same rate of inflation. It's been said that we're either coming out of a storm, in a storm, or going into a storm but we can drastically reduce the chances of a financial storm or transform the storm into a light drizzle if we better prepare ourselves. We've already covered the importance of saving for an emergency fund in the planning chapter, along with how much money you should save and the contributing factors of that decision but before we look at the various *ways* we can save money, let me just say there is a difference between saving and investing. Saving means protecting your money from loss and storing or preserving money for later needs. Investing means putting money into a vehicle you believe will make you more money and one way most people do that is through the stock market. Growth is not guaranteed however due to the risk of unpredictable markets.

There are various vehicles in which to save or invest money and just as many catchy phrases to help you remember--Pay yourself first, Make it automatic, Diversify, etc. As far as investing, there are stocks, bonds, mutual funds, index funds, IRAs, Roth IRAs, real estate, the list goes on. There are also tax advantages that you should be aware of, some are immediate while others are deferred until retirement age. Since most of these financial vehicles cross the road from savings to investing and because there is too much information to cover in one chapter on the many types of financial investment vehicles, I suggest you talk to an accountant, financial advisor, or investment broker. For this chapter, I will concentrate on saving in general.

The first step to saving money is making the decision to do so. You have to make up your mind that having money in savings is more of a priority than your next frivolous purchase. So how do you save money? One way is to make it seamless and "easy," make it automatic. You can elect to have your bank automatically transfer a certain amount of money from your checking account every month and deposit it directly into your savings account which is "paying yourself first." Just as the government automatically takes Medicare and Medicaid out of each paycheck before you see one dime, you can do the same thing for your own benefit. Just as you watch the Medicaid amount grow with each paycheck and are amazed come year end of how much money you have unwillingly, but automatically contributed, you can do the same thing for yourself—willingly.

How do you find the money? You can adjust your expectations and live without ten or twenty dollars a paycheck or whatever amount you decide to make automatic. This is the same process used with 401k contributions but your savings account is readily accessible. If you prefer not to utilize this automatic feature, you can do this manually on the first of every month, each paycheck, or every time you pay your tithes you can then write out a check to go into your savings. If you decide to do this manually, the watchout is that you not only have to remember to do it but you also have to constantly decide to continue versus deciding one time to set it up and going on with life. As discussed earlier, when this is allocated in your monthly budget, you can't help but to do it. Whatever process you use, just make it work for you and stick to it. Even though it may take some time you will eventually see your savings increase and before long you will have saved more money than you ever thought was practical for you.

You can also accelerate your savings by earning more money and saving it or spending less money by cutting expenses and saving it. You can earn more by temporarily getting a second job or working more overtime. You can offer a service like house cleaning or cutting grass on your days off. Things you can do that have the same effect of earning more money is selling stuff. Here are some tips to do so:

- Sell stuff on Craigslist, Ebay, or online community garage sales in your area
- Sell stuff at traditional community garage sales or an individual one. Some local papers will list it for free. Make sure the price of your items are clearly marked, which increases your chance of selling them.
- Consignment at clothing stores and resale shops

Now that we've explored ways to save, let's look at ways to cut expenses so that you'll have more money to save.

Cash is King

You probably have heard the saying, "Cash is King." Buying things in cash can not only deter you from buying more than you need but can also influence a seller to lower the price of an item you plan to buy. It is now the practice of some retailers to give 5-10% discounts for cash customers. This works in your favor and leads to money savings. This applies to large purchases such as cars and smaller purchases like furniture. As a buyer, you have more leverage and negotiating power when you are carrying cash. You can negotiate from a point of strength and are more apt to name your own price. Try taking cash the next time you go shopping.

Not only can you get huge discounts by buying with cash, but you also minimize how much money you spend. Paying with cash psychologically causes you to spend less money because there's more of an emotional connection attached to paying with cash than it is with a credit or even debit card, because you physically see the green bills leaving your hands, your possession. So if you want to save more money by spending less and receiving bigger discounts, buy like a king—with cash.

Convenience costs

Another way you can save money is realizing that there is a cost for convenience. Normally the things we buy that make our lives more convenient cost more. By convenient I'm referring to items or services that save us time, or make life easier. You only need to go to a convenience store, c-store, to see what I'm talking about. The prices at a c-store or gas station, as some would refer to it, are typically higher than what you'd find in a grocery store. Take a bottle of Gatorade for instance. The price of a 32oz bottle of Gatorade at a supermarket can range from $1.00-$1.29 or more depending on whether it's in season or not, summer or winter. That same exact bottle would cost $1.49-$1.89 or more at a gas station. Why? You're paying for convenience. The gas station will typically have shorter checkout lines and the customer usually buys items for immediate consumption. In the case of Gatorade, it is stocked in the cooler door at the C-store versus on the grocery shelf at the supermarket; being cold you plan to drink it as soon as you get to your car. There are times when a C-store runs a promotion that decreases the price to the same or better than what you'd find at the grocery store but that can be sporadic. There are benefits to paying more for convenience, but be aware of the differences in costs and weigh rather the convenience is worth the higher cost for you. Does saving $0.50-$1.00 on an item sound trivial? That's only an example of one item. Multiply that by the amount of items you'd typically buy on a grocery shopping trip and you've just added $50 to $75 to your bill. True, there aren't too many people that would shop for groceries at a gas station but the same principle applies to a drug store. Again, you pay for convenience.

Transfer that concept to a restaurant or fast food establishment. Your food bill will look a lot different if you eat out every day for a month rather than stocking up on food items at your neighborhood market. Not only do you see a difference in costs between fast food and grocery, but also amongst the items found within the grocery or mass merchandise store. You will pay more for ready-to-eat items than you will for traditional meals. Meals that require you to actually cook them in the oven or on the stove generally cost less than their microwaveable counterparts. Not only are you sacrificing money for the quicker meals, but sometimes nutritional value as well. Normally the ready-made, throw-in-the-microwave meals have lost some nutritional value due to over processing. Along with full meals, hand-picked vegetables take longer to prepare than the frozen or canned vegetables. In the instance of vegetables however it actually may be cheaper to buy the more processed food, so your cost may not be felt in the form of cash but nutrition. Either way you will pay in some form or fashion for convenience.

Insurances

You want to save money on your material things as well. Make sure you take the necessary steps to protect the assets that you've worked so hard to accumulate over the years by insuring them. The most common insurances are for your home and automobiles but don't forget about renters insurance for apartment renters and I already mentioned GAP insurance for those who are paying on their cars. More important than protecting your material accumulations, you need to protect your most important asset—your income.

Beyond health insurance, make sure you have an ample amount of disability insurance as well. Disability insurance is often overlooked and underinsured. Many of us believe we are invincible and that injuries only happen to other people. If we do elect it, many of us choose the lowest coverage offered under our employer's plan just so we have it, yet if we really were to become injured, the low percentage we elected would not be able to meet our basic income needs. Applicable to all insurances, do your research. Be careful when choosing your home and car insurances; the most advertised plan can be the most expensive and the most vulnerable to become bankrupt if a major disaster occurs. Cute pets and celebrities are expensive spokesmen and the more money a company pays in advertising and marketing, the pricier your insurance can cost.

Wills

In the same vein of insurance are wills, advance directives and trusts. These are designed to protect your assets and comply with your wishes. There are essentially two wills to consider having, a living will and a last will. When people talk about making out their will, they are typically referring to the last will, which is exercised once you die, but a living will is used while you are alive. A living will specifies your desire regarding medical care and things like life support in the event you are too ill to communicate. Another consideration in a living will is designating a Power of Attorney, who will handle your legal and financial matters. You may choose which areas they will be able to make decisions over and the duration of their appointment. A last will is for giving out property and establishing guardianship for children. One thing to consider if you or your spouse have other children outside of the marriage, the court will separate 50% of the community property equally between all children unless the parent's last will says otherwise.

Similar to a last will, a living trust is also used to distribute property. One difference in a last will and a living trust is that a trust can issue property faster by avoiding probate court, and will do so privately in the case of your death. You want to avoid probate court if possible because an estate can be tied up in probate for up to three years and can cost in the thousands in fees in a worst case scenario. Attorneys fees alone associated with probate court can range from $125-$300 an hour. You can also avoid probate court if your estate is valued under the statutory minimum for your state, which is $50,000 for Texas, or having a small-estate affidavit filed. There are so many nuances to wills, advance directives, and trusts that I suggest you consult an attorney with your wishes.

But I'm Rich

I want to focus for a moment on the population of people who are financially rich. If you are rich, again I say congratulations. God has blessed you with wonderful opportunities. Your hard work has paid off and your sacrifices to ensure yourself the life you've envisioned were worth the financial freedom you now enjoy. The watchout is to make sure you keep what you've worked so hard to establish. We've all heard the stories of rich people who've lost everything. There's probably more sure ways to lose money than it is to accumulate money so being rich is not a guarantee or prerequisite to keeping your riches.

Being inattentive can cost you money. Some rich people think they have so much money so they don't have to pay attention to it, but having more money does not exempt you from being responsible over it. The more money you have, the more you will spend, and the more watchful eye you need to have. Also, being too trusting to people on your payroll, like your accountant or lawyer can add to expenses, hence drain your finances. You may be tempted to hire an accountant and place all your trust in that person. You may want to just pay them, forget about the details, and enjoy life completely care-free. You sign whatever your accountant puts in front of you without asking questions, ignoring the fact that no one is going to care more about your money than you. Don't just sign documents without reading and clearly understanding the wording of what you sign. Take the time to look up words you do not understand the full meaning of, because you could be giving away your fortune. You also must remember that you are still held accountable for the decisions your accountant makes on your behalf. It takes less time to lose money than it did to earn it. It may take years to amass a fortune but only seconds to lose it so since you've got it, do all you can to preserve what your hard work has produced. You need to inspect what you expect.

Expenses

In order to keep as much of your money as possible, you must decrease your expenses. In line with the quote that preceded this chapter, wealth is a result of what you get to keep. There is an inverse relationship in wealth increasing as our expenses decrease and one of the biggest expenses, not assets, for most people is their homes. No matter your social or financial status, a house can be the number one drain on your money. Notwithstanding the fact that many people have bought homes they can't truly afford, a house has many expenses beyond just the mortgage note as previously discussed. For the rich, it is important to get a home and property that you can maintain on your income after your career is over. Just the upkeep on million-dollar homes is staggering. Please understand that you can have a paid-off house and still not be able to afford the upkeep. Why do you think celebrities, sports figures, and the like go bankrupt after they've been out of the game for a while? There truly are many contributing factors but it's important to adjust your lifestyle to your "post-game" status. Don't base the size of your house on the wages you are earning at the height of your career. This can be hard to sustain. Beyond your home, your money can quickly dwindle away on expenses such as private jets, extravagant parties, and bad investments.

Everyone, rich and non-rich alike may need to reduce expenses. If you dread the thought of reducing expenses, be creative. Think of it as a game, or just embrace the challenge. This does not have to be permanent. This can be a temporary reduction until you get where you want to be financially, you can always readjust later. You can reward yourself for each milestone you pass by taking one of the sacrifices off of your list. For example, after you pay off that last debt you can start going to the movies again, etc.

To get you started, here is a list of ways to reduce expenses:

- Decrease the deductions on your pay check so you don't get a big tax refund at the end of the year. This will increase your take-home pay each pay period and you can pay off debt and interest with this increase during the year rather than struggling all year while giving the government an interest-free loan that they just give back to you in the form of an income tax refund check.
- Check your employer for discounts on things like cell phones, insurance, daycare, and memberships based on their vendor partnerships
- Utilize your health and dependent care reserve accounts which reduce your taxable income
- Get your medicine prescriptions through the mail at a reduced cost vs traditional pharmacies
- Go to the dollar movie theatre or rent movies for free at the library
- Rent books and music CD's at the library vs buying them
- Take your lunch to work vs eating out
- Buy generic grocery and household items vs name brand
- Buy used clothes at thrift stores, resale shops, or garage sales
- Extend the time between hair and nail appointments
- Switch from department store make-up to a less expensive brand

- Switch skin care systems to more natural or less expensive choices like using witch hazel as an astringent

The Lottery Curse

Please don't be one of the ones who save and cut expenses only to use the extra money to buy as many lottery tickets as possible with the hopes of striking it rich or putting it all on red #23 on the roulette wheel. There's nothing wrong with either, in the casual sense. I know others may not agree and some of you are cringing as I say this but the lottery and casino, are close cousins to the stock market and the raffle ticket you buy from the little league team or the church to win that prize. Really, what's the difference? The act is essentially the same, you are giving money for a chance, not a guarantee, to win something. Just because an organization or institution calls it a donation, doesn't make it any different.

Granted you can get addicted to gambling at the casino, which is very unlikely buying raffle tickets yet they are both based on taking a chance, giving your money and taking a chance that you will win something in return. I've probably "lost" more money on raffle tickets than someone else has "lost" playing the lottery. Why do I even talk about this? I just want you to realize that odds are, you will not strike it rich playing the lottery or spending your weekends at the casino. I've never seen a person make it on the Forbes list doing either. The Bible talks about such rapid gain.

A hard worker has plenty of food, but a person who chases fantasies has no sense. Proverbs 12:11 New Living Translation

Many lottery recipients are worse off financially *after* their winnings than before. If you can't manage a little money, you definitely can't manage a lot of money. So don't overindulge in the lottery, get-rich-quick schemes, or anything else that seems too good to be true because you probably know that it is.

Things To Remember

- The Ant
- Financial Auto Pilot
- Saving vs Investing
- Automatic vs Manual
- Convenience Costs
- Insurance
- Last vs Living will
- Reduce Expenses

More Saving Scriptures

The wise store up choice food and olive oil, but fools gulp theirs down. Proverbs 21:20 NIV

Dishonest money dwindles away, but whoever gathers money little by little makes it grow. Proverbs 13:11 NIV

They should collect all the food of these good years that are coming and store up the grain under the authority of Pharaoh, to be kept in the cities for food. This food should be held in reserve for the country, to be used during the seven years of famine that will come upon Egypt, so that the country may not be ruined by the famine. Genesis 41:35-36 NIV

Know your sheep by name; carefully attend to your flocks; (Don't take them for granted; possessions don't last forever, you know.) And then, when the crops are in and the harvest is stored in the barns, You can knit sweaters from lambs' wool, and sell your goats for a profit; There will be plenty of milk and meat to last your family through the winter. Proverbs 27: 23-27 The Message Bible

For where your treasure is, there will your heart be also. Matthew 6:21 KJV

A good man leaveth an inheritance to his children's children: and the wealth of the sinner is laid up for the just. Proverbs 13:22 KJV

The blessing of the Lord, it maketh rich, and he addeth no sorrow with it. Proverbs 10:22 KJV

Invest in seven ventures, yes, in eight; you do not know what disaster may come upon the land. Ecclesiastes 11:2 NIV

God wants us to change the world, not conform to it.
—**Shalonda McFarland**

Chapter Seven
(NO PUN INTENDED)
Borrowing

Robbing Peter to Pay Paul

The rich ruleth over the poor, and the borrower is servant to the lender.
Proverbs 22:7 KJV

And be not conformed to this world: but be ye transformed by the renewing of your mind, that ye may prove what is that good, and acceptable, and perfect, will of God.
Romans 12:2 KJV

Even though our dollar bills still say In God We Trust, our actions as a people, a nation, and even as Christians, say otherwise. We have become a people that buy on a whim, whether we have the money to pay for it or not. We have more balances on our credit cards than we do in our savings accounts. We have let our guards down and have allowed ourselves to be deceived by companies pushing their own product and their own agenda at our expense.

The sad thing is, when it comes to debt, there is not much difference between Christians and the world. On the job, Christian and non-Christian co-workers are having the same money problems. The world can't come to you for advice because you are in the same mess they are in. This is not a very good witness. Christians should be able to give the world good, sound biblical advice about any and every issue in life, including financial. Sadly, most Christians can't offer such advice because we don't know what The Word says about a situation and even if we did know, the majority of us wouldn't follow it anyway. We spend more time eating off of the world's table that we are too full to even think of eating off of God's table. We have steadily placed our trust and confidence in this world that we ignore the Word of God. I'm definitely not picking on you. I've been there myself. I know how it feels to hear people talking about their money problems and feeling embarrassed because I'm secretly experiencing the same issues. I remember the frustration I felt knowing that my finances were in disarray. I had mismanaged my money and I was the only one to blame. We have forgotten that God supplies our need and we have placed our trust in borrowing, mainly through credit cards, and say *that* can supply our need (and greed). So have you transferred your trust from God to your credit card? Is it even possible to live without a credit card? Is there anything wrong with credit cards anyway?

As far as deciding if credit cards are wrong, we need to see what the Word says about them. Of course The Bible doesn't explicitly say in quotes that credit cards are wrong just as it doesn't spell out every thing or every situation that we face in today's society—like cars, the space shuttle, or microwaves. You have to take the lessons and principles the Bible teaches and apply them to a specific situation. So credit cards are not stated in the Bible but borrowing is. The Bible does warn us in Proverbs 22:7 about the dangers of borrowing money which is what credit cards are all about. When the Word says that the borrower is servant to the lender, that's exactly what it means. If you have a credit card, you are a servant to the company whose logo the card bears and in due time that same card will own you. The credit card companies' whole purpose is for you and I to consistently borrow money.

There are many reasons we as a people use credit cards. Many of us use it simply because it is the accepted and "normal" practice in today's culture. It's easy to find yourself with many cards. You get one for the gas rebate, another for the cash-back bonus, airline miles, your favorite department store, a separate one issued from your bank…the list goes on. Some on the other hand think we can't live without one, or two, or three of them. Here are three myths of why some of us believe we must have a credit card:

1. I need one for emergencies.
2. I need one to rent a car or book a hotel.
3. I need one to buy items in case I have a dispute over charges.

Well, let me tell you that it is possible to live without a credit card. I am proof that it can be done. Here are the facts that debunk the preceding three myths:

1. A savings account, or money market account should be your emergency fund. You can consistently put money into an emergency fund at your local bank and build up the balance so that you will not need a credit card.
2. You can use a debit card to rent a car or book a hotel. Yes, the hotel may place a dollar amount hold on the card, but if you can not afford the hold, can you really afford the hotel stay in the first place?
3. Most debit cards have the same dispute guarantee that credit cards have.

So, I've debunked the myth that you <u>must</u> have a credit card to make it in this society. But some do not use credit cards because they think they have to, but because they *want* to. You might be thinking, "I get so many perks for using my card. What's the problem?"

The scripture found in Proverbs 22:7 is there to warn us of what is attached to borrowing—bondage. The Bible does not say the borrower is not a servant to the lender *if* they pay back the money each month. The Bible does say that the borrower is servant to the lender, period. This is a statement with no limitations or qualifying situations.

What is a servant? A servant is defined as one that performs duties for the person or home of a master or personal employer. There are different kinds of servants but I'll focus on one in particular—a bond servant. A bond servant is someone who is bound to service without wages or pay. This is a slave. So replace the word *servant* with the word *slave*. Now the scripture reads, "the borrower is slave to the lender" and some of us are slaves to our MasterCard.

A slave has no say so, he must do what his master tells him to. Are you a slave? Here are three signs that you may be one:

1. You do not have the money to pay off the credit card(s) you have.
2. You are constantly doing balance transfers to get lower interest rates.
3. You can not resist the new credit card offers that come in the mail.

Don't beat yourself up about being in debt. Credit card companies spend a ton of money studying our buying habits and tendencies. They take that knowledge and devise ways to get us to use their cards but a credit card is a false sense of security. We feel honored when we get a letter stating we are preapproved for a credit line of $5,000 based on our good use of credit. What they really mean is that they see you continue to borrow and they want a piece of the action and are betting that you'll get your credit card balance high enough where you won't be able to pay it off during the grace period, and therefore accrue interest charges that will make the company rich.

How did I get Here?

How did your Master(card) lure you? What enticing offer did the credit card company get you with? Did they offer you 25% off of your purchase if you "just sign up right now" for this department store card? Was it 5% cash back for each dollar you spend? Do you even realize that in order to get $100 back in cash you would have to spend $2000 on that card (5% of $2000)? Or was your enticement a measly T-shirt or hat worth $4.99? Think about what bait was used to get you hooked. Some people have over $10,000 in credit card debt that started because of an innocent offer.

College Credit

The college campus is the place where many of us were introduced to credit cards. By then you are 18 years old and finally an adult and you feel you are on your own. You can now make independent decisions and getting a credit card seems like your proof of maturity. You probably were introduced through a peer at a table set up near the student union, approved and endorsed by the college campus, and all you had to do was fill out an application the size of a postcard. You completed it between classes and walked away with a cool t-shirt or hat and the confidence in knowing you were deemed worthy to be offered a ticket into adulthood.

Some parents even urge their college-bound graduates by saying, "It's time for you to build your credit." This typically means a department store credit card with a minimal limit. You may even feel disappointed when you're only approved for a $300 limit but you quickly discover that when you charge something and pay it off, your credit line increases. This seems like a reward so you keep using and charging up the card, and a cycle has begun. The higher the credit limit, the more responsible and empowered you feel. This of course is a false sense of responsibility.

After you've had this card for a length of time, you magically start receiving more offers from different creditors who all want to reward you for being such a responsible adult and you can't turn down a reward. In fact you're preapproved because you are so special and the more offers you get and accept the more trustworthy you feel you are. You think, "Of course they wouldn't offer me something I couldn't afford so since they feel I can afford it, I'll keep using it." We throw common sense out the window. Since the companies feel you are trustworthy you begin to use their cards more often and charge higher amounts until one day you can't keep up.

The time will come when you can't pay off the entire balance before the due date. Something will inevitably come up that will interfere with your charge-and-pay-off cycle. You'll either forget to make the payment, mail the payment in a day late, or have competing obligations that month. Something will occur that will throw a monkey wrench into your well-oiled machine.

Credit card companies not only want us to use their cards, but they want us to be dependent on their cards. They want us to accumulate so much debt that we can't pay it off. You probably did not get caught up in debt overnight, so it may take some time to get out of it. Be encouraged, it can be done! You first have to decide that you will do it. In that decision though, must come the commitment not to use credit cards again. No new charges. Seriously, how bad do you want to be free? Take a stand and get rid of the credit cards! Start using debit cards or carrying real money, you know the green paper bills. Let's get reacquainted with real money again.

When you look at paper money, what do you see? There are many differences depending on what money denomination you are looking at. The presidents' faces are different according to the dollar amount, and the pictures are different on the back. Let me give you a quick run through of what you may not even realize. On the front of a one dollar bill is the picture of our first president, George Washington, on the back are two pictures of The Great Seal of The United States. The two dollar bill has Thomas Jefferson on the front and a replica of a painting "The Declaration of Independence" by John Trumbull on the back. The five dollar bill has Abraham Lincoln on the front, and The Lincoln Memorial on the back. The ten dollar bill has Alexander Hamilton (a non-president) on the front and The U.S. Treasury building on the back. Can you guess what's on the twenty dollar bill? Andrew Jackson is on the front and The White House is on the back. Yes, I'm going to tell you all of them. I know you're intrigued. (Excuse me while I go to the bank to get a fifty and one hundred dollar bill. I do not keep that kind of cash on me.)

O.K. The fifty has Ulysses Grant on the front and the U.S. Capitol on the back. The one hundred dollar bill has Benjamin Franklin (a non-president) on the front and Independence Hall on the back. Despite the many differences on paper money, there are some similarities. Along with the words, "Federal Reserve Note" and "The United States Of America" the phrase I like is "In God We Trust." The phrase is not "In credit we trust" yet we as Christians have bought off on the myth that we need a credit card to survive. Again, credit card companies pay a lot of money in marketing and advertising to make us believe they are the ones we should put our trust in. We see ads that say, "Life takes Visa." No, life takes God. The next time you think, look at, or use a credit card, look at the front and see if *it* says, "In God We Trust." Every time you use one you are in essence saying, "I don't trust you God, I trust this credit card." David Bach in his book *Start Late, Finish Rich* calls credit cards liability cards. I call them servant cards and slave cards.

Wait! What about...

You may be thinking, you have to keep a credit card because you just can't give up the perks--free airline miles, free gas, discounts, etc. I felt the same way. Let me ask you something. Why do you think the credit card companies offer these traps, temptations, I mean incentives? Remember that they are in business to make money. They are not altruistic. Keep in mind the saying, If it sounds too good to be true, then it is.

I thought I could get over on the credit card companies. I would use them for the perks and thought

I was making money. I thought I was really smart. I used my Discover card for the one percent back, and because the statement would group my spending into categories. I even convinced my husband to only use our Discover card for each and every purchase. I knew in order to maximize the 1% cash back benefit, I'd have to rack up a hefty balance. (You'd have to charge $1000 to get $10 back at the 1% rate.) They'd have special months where you could earn 2%. I wanted to make sure I spent a lot to get the most money back, that way we would beat the system and make more money. Does this sound crazy to you? Apparently it doesn't, because most Americans get too easily trapped into this cycle. You can not beat someone at their own game and the credit card companies invented the game.

Debt-The Big Three

Credit cards, automobiles, and mortgages are the top three debts, in the order of how most people acquire them. We've talked about credit cards, so now let's look at the next two debts and examine how much of a negative impact they can have on your finances.

Automobiles

Having a car note is a way of life these days. Says who? The auto manufacturers and anyone who hasn't done it any other way perpetrate this myth. We don't even think about whether to have a note or not. We go on autopilot and just get one. It takes most people three to five years to pay a car off and then soon after that, they go get another vehicle and sign up for another note. It's like living your life in three to five year jail sentences. Let me tell you it is possible to buy a car without going into debt to do it. It may take time and you may not be able to afford the car you want but the car you need. And all we really need is a vehicle to get us from point A to point B.

That's it. I told you about my first car. Now let me tell you about my fourth car, which I financed. I was in my early twenties and decided I would go down to the car lot by myself and trade in my old vehicle, which was on its last leg, for a nice used one. I told my dad that I could handle it because I had researched the type of vehicle I wanted. I ended up getting a nice vehicle but at a 12% interest rate. Come to find out, my credit history was not established enough so I had to get a higher rate, or so they said. I thought about it and decided that since I was still living at home, I could pay the car off quickly so the interest rate didn't matter. Hah! Although I researched the vehicle, I did not have enough research on life. And life happened. It ended up taking me a number of years to pay the car off. Needless to say, the finance company made a lot of money on me.

This is one reason why I utilize what one might call the three-day rule. Before making any major purchase, wait three days before you finalize the deal. I'm not talking about one day deciding you need another vehicle and then three days later picking one out. I'm talking about waiting three days after you've already picked out, test drove, and gotten the cash together to close the deal. You will avoid many poor decisions if you first slow down and think things through. I'm not talking about rationalizing your purchase decision, which is what most of us do when we make a decision on the show-room floor. You need time away from the place of purchase when you make your decision. Salespeople are continuously trained to sell and they've practiced many tactics to get you to buy now.

Let's face it, most of the time we're hoping to be talked into something we want—the upgrade, the package options, but this is not the time to be talked into something by someone who will benefit financially from your decision. You need time to think. If I would have waited three days before buying my vehicle, I would not have accepted the 12% interest offered me. Many of us make the same poor choice I did. We make a large purchase decision in less than three hours and it affects us for over three years. To avoid all this, know your parameters before you go. Know what is a must have, a nice to have, and what you are willing to pay for each. This is especially the case when you still choose to finance rather than pay in cash. You must realize that everything you add to the vehicle in terms of optional equipment will increase the purchase price and will also be financed at the agreed upon rate. Know the range of interest rate you will accept. Understand their return policy. Some states require companies to give their customers three days to return a purchase if they change their minds. And by all means, be willing to walk away and know what your walk-away point is.

To avoid debt, save up enough money to buy a vehicle in cash. You might not be able to afford what you want right now but you can make preparations now to get it later. You may have to get a $500 cash car or clunker until you can save up enough money to upgrade to something better. Be content and drive that car until the wheels fall off then take the money you have been saving and purchase a better car. Keep saving and upgrading until you get what you want.

You can save money quickly when you're not making monthly payments and paying interest on a vehicle.

Also, extend the life of your vehicles. If the vehicle is safe to drive, which is the number one priority, its looks are a distant second. Make improvements to it, do minor repairs, and keep it moving. When the kids on the bus were laughing at my car because the interior roof lining was torn and sagging, instead of getting the inside done, I put tacks all around the top. Nobody would be able to see that unless they rode in the car. So for less than $2, I fixed an aesthetic problem rather than paying hundreds to a professional or rushing to the car lot for a newer model.

Furthermore, be careful not to take your car so seriously. It's just a car. Most of us drive automobiles that go down in value with every mile we add to them. Don't go to extremes to keep your car updated with the newest technology and adding upgrades that don't necessarily increase the value of the car but increases its likelihood of being stolen, ie) expensive visual and audio equipment, electronics, and rims. The absurd thing is that a lot of people make all of these expensive "enhancements" on a car that they don't even own yet. They are still paying the note on the car and now have a note on the rims as well. So to avoid car debt, live with contentment, preparation, and patience.

Mortgages

The same formula that helps you avoid car debt also applies to home loans. It is best to avoid a mortgage but most of us don't have the patience or will to wait the 8 to 10 years or more that it would take to save up enough money to buy a house in cash. It would take more or less time depending on how disciplined you are saving money and whether or not you are overcome by the temptation to buy a new car or a new whatever with the money you've saved. We're not big on delayed gratification but if we did delay gratification in the short run we would save ourselves thousands of dollars in the long run. For example, if you bought a home for $125,000 you can actually pay over $125,000 just in interest charges alone on a 30-year note depending on the interest rate. The amount you actually pay all together is more to the tune of $250,000. I can't believe this is legal, and more unbelievable is the fact that society accepts this as the norm and we continue to be held in bondage as we make payment after payment. If you indeed have a mortgage, the best thing to do is pay it off early by paying down the principle every month. You don't need to pay a fee and get on the mortgage company's program to do this. Do it yourself by adding extra money to the principle each month and making sure the mortage company applies it correctly on your statement.

Asset or Liability

People get mortgages that are too expensive and get them too early. One reason is because they look at a house as an asset rather than a liability. I've always heard that a house is an asset, the biggest asset some will ever own. Really? What is an asset? An asset is defined as something you own that you can convert to cash and a liability as what you owe. Simply put, an asset makes you money and a liability loses you money. Miss a few mortgage payments and you'll find out which category a house falls in. Lending companies are quick to point out that you are throwing away money every month in the form of rent if you don't have a mortgage but don't call attention to the money you lose in interest every month if you do have a mortgage. When my husband and I bought our home, we lost more money in monthly interest than we did on rent money. As was our case, most people should stay renters longer. Oftentimes people lose less money renting an apartment than they do "owning" a home. Even if your current apartment rent is more than your future monthly mortgage payment, you must consider all the costs of owning a home to do a fair comparison. If you don't consider all factors, you will get a house that is too expensive for you.

I've explained how people get mortgages that are too expensive; now let me explain how they get them too early. If you have other debt, ie) student loans, car loans, or credit cards, then you need to wait and pay these off before adding another debt to your balance sheet. I say this because evidently you can't even afford to pay your current loans, which is why you still have them, so what makes you think you can add another enormous debt to your plate? That's like asking you to add a bowling ball to your juggling act when you can't even handle the four plastic mini balls, or debts, already in your routine. Picture a clown in the middle of a juggling act with plastic balls then adding a bowling ball to the mix. That's virtually impossible yet that's what a lot of us do when we don't take the time to evaluate where we are financially before we add more complexity to the equation. We attempt to do the impossible and wonder why we are stressed and why our health suffers.

Don't expect a mortgage lender to let you know you can't afford something. They just want to make the sale and would rather raise your interest rate than tell you no. They'll take as much money from you as they can, knowing they'll eventually have the house back anyway after you foreclose, hence the housing bubble that we're in now.

Cash-Flow House

Regardless of your thoughts on if your house is an asset or liability, some companies have discovered how to further get money out of you by telling you that your home can generate cash flow utilizing reverse mortgages and home equity lines of credit. I'll briefly explain the differences in them. If you are considering one of these, keep in mind that like all debt, know what you're getting into. Both plans use the equity in your home. For an equity line of credit you receive a lump sum of money and then pay monthly installments back to the bank but in a reverse mortgage the bank pays the person back and a lump sum is one of three ways to do so; the other two options are monthly payments or a credit line. Also, you must be at least 62 years old to qualify for a reverse mortgage, there are no age limitations with an equity line of credit. Reverse mortgages require little credit check and you can receive monthly payments as long as you live, or use the home as a permanent residence. You won't end up being upside down with it as the case with many car loans either.

With both options you can keep your home if you pay the money back. The reason why people consider these is the need for money—a reverse mortgage if you are older and can't afford to make your mortgage payments, the equity line of credit if you *can* make payments. The interest on reverse mortgages is not tax deductible unless you pay off some or all of the loan, it is tax deductible on the equity line of credit.

Now you know just enough to be dangerous. If you are contemplating either of these, you need to get counseling first.

The big three—credit cards, automobiles, and mortgages may be the biggest ticket items or most popular things that cause one to go in and stay in debt but unfortunately they are not the only sources of borrowing, since there are many reasons why people borrow money.

One person pretends to be rich, yet has nothing; another pretends to be poor, yet has great wealth. Proverbs 13:7 NIV

Some people live the same cycle that they saw growing up, the vicious poverty cycle lined with poor choices and little opportunities, and example after example of others' failures as a constant, immovable glass ceiling that seems unbreakable. Life does not have to be this way. God designed for you to have an abundant life.

In order to live the abundant life God planned for us, we must follow the roadmap he's already established. The quickest journey to that life is debt-free living. Debt free means no debt at all…no car payments, no student loan payments, no payday loans, no mortgage payments, etc. Make the decision to try God. Rely on Him and watch His Word come to pass.

Getting out of Debt

Good things begin to happen once you make the decision that you will not rely on debt. If you want G.O.O.D. things to happen, then you need to Get Out

Of Debt. So do you really want to Get Out Of Debt and stay out? The reality of being debt-free may seem like a fantasy right now but if you focus your energy and use discipline, you CAN be debt free. Just think how nice it will feel not to have any payments. I did not say any bills, because we'll always have bills to pay if we want to use services like electricity, water, and heat but I'm talking about no payments, like something you bought on "credit" that you have to pay down every month before you own it.

What would you do with the $400 or $500 a month that you now are giving to the car dealership and finance company to help pay their salespeople's salaries? Would you save more, give more? Let's look at this a different way. What would you do if you lost your job? If you think it's hard to make your payments now, how much harder would it be with no income? How long would you be able to make monthly payments to all your creditors with no income coming in? How many months would it take to find another job in this economy? How many paychecks are you from being broke? I hope I have your attention. Well, here's how to get out of debt.

First, save up $500-$1000 and put it into a separate savings account at your bank. You want to have access to it in case of an emergency but you do not want to have it in your checking account because you'll spend it. The goal is $1000 but in an extreme case save a minimum of $500. This is your emergency fund, rainy day fund, or whatever you want to call it. This will immediately break your dependence on a credit card.

This may take a few months to do but do this as fast as you can. How? Stop buying nice to haves, and stick with necessities. Stop going out to eat, do not buy that present, do not buy those concert tickets, cancel that subscription, etc. You can cut something that you do not need to get the money. (Review the ideas I gave on cutting expenses.) Another option is temporarily decreasing your 401k contributions only to the portion that the company matches. Get a second job, or have a garage sale, just be creative. Now that you have this money, you do not need to depend on a credit card or payday loan for emergencies.

Second, cut up your credit cards but continue to pay the bill every month. Yes, cut them up so you will not have the temptation, but don't actually close your accounts until you have a zero balance. (Keep your statements and record the three-digit security code found on the back of the card in a secure place). I do not care how many airline miles you get or how much cash back you get for each dollar you spend. It is all a gimmick to keep you using their card. The credit card company must be getting something out of it right? Why do you think they are being so "generous" to you? Companies are in business to make money. So ask yourself how are they making money off of me? Even if you pay your balance in full every month, you can not beat them at their own game. Something will happen. The cards are stacked in their favor so stop playing their game. We've already discussed this.

Third, write down all your debts, everything you owe, so you can focus on paying them all off. (We'll tackle the mortgage later). Experts vary somewhat on how to list your debts. Should you list them by interest rate or by amount? Logically, you would think interest rate (pay off the debt with the highest *interest* rate first) but that is not the case. In reality, paying off the debt with the lowest *balance* first works faster, for I've tried both methods. You will pay off your debts faster this way because you see the results quicker. Then your emotions kick in, you gain momentum, and you keep paying off debts even faster.

For example, let's say you have three debts--$50 at 5% interest, $100 at 10%, and $150 at 15%. The quickest way to pay them off is to pay the $50 bill first, regardless of the interest rate, then the $100, and then the $150. If you have monthly payments on all three you would pay the minimum balance on all and you would pay extra money (as much as you can afford) on the $50 (the smallest bill). You would continue this until the $50 bill was paid in full. Then you would take the payment you used to put on the $50 bill and apply it plus the minimum payment to the $100 bill, and so on and so on until you have paid your last (and largest) debt in full. How long will this take? That depends on how badly you want to get out of debt. It truly depends on you!

Recap

- Start an Emergency Fund of $1000.
- Cut up all your credit cards at one time or one by one after you have paid off the balance and cancelled each account.
- Pay off all debts from smallest amount to largest (Temporarily decrease retirement contributions to only what the company matches).

Next Steps

- Increase Your Emergency Fund-Keep putting the same amount of money that you were having to pay on debt, into savings each month until you have 3 to 6 months worth of expenses saved.

- Fund Your Business or Dream-If you are planning on starting a business, start saving money in another account to help launch your start-up.
- Retirement-Now increase your retirement contribution to its previous percentage.
- Mortgage-Pay off your mortgage by applying more money to principle each month.

More Help

Some people have caused so much damage to their credit and are so far in debt that they feel they need outside help. There are companies, profit and non-profit, that offer legitimate products and/or services to help you with your finances. Let me caution you in saying that very few are necessary. What I mean by that is these products may be a convenience and may save you time but they will charge you a fee to do something you can do yourself for free. Two of the most used services are credit repair and debt consolidation. Credit repair companies claim they can fix your credit, yet they cannot legally change or delete legitimate "bad items" on your report. Let me just say that you do not need a credit repair service to help restore your credit and there are no "secrets" to repairing your credit. Some companies will charge you hundreds to thousands of dollars for something that you can do yourself. What they may do is refute or question items on your report to one of the credit bureaus who will in turn contact each company in question and tell them to provide proof of the derogatory claim within thirty days or they will delete the item from your report. You can contact the credit bureau yourself and do that. You can also check for errors in address, length of time accounts have been open, account balances, credit limits, etc. Correcting errors and removing derogatory history from your credit report is what can improve your credit score. We'll look at more ways to improve your score in another section. Again, this is something you can do yourself for free. I briefly told you what a credit repair service will do, now let's look at the other type of help—debt consolidation.

Credit repair services will focus on increasing your credit score while debt consolidation will try to keep you current and paying your bills on time. A debt consolidation company will have you gather all your bills and roll them into one bill with one monthly payment. You pay them the total amount due of all your bills and add their fee and they proceed to pay your creditors one by one. Once more you can perform both of these services yourself for free. Be very careful if you do choose to use one of these services. This industry has a lot of fraudalent companies in it, so make sure you read and understand the terms and get all their fees in writing.

Damaging your credit was a process and so is repairing it which takes time and a commitment. First, have the right mindset that you do owe the money and should want to be a man of your word and pay every penny back, especially if your bills are due to poor choices. There are circumstances however where people got in a jam due to unforeseen medical bills or extended lengths of time when they were out of work which caused a financial meltdown. This can easily happen. One spell of sickness that is not covered under your insurance can wipe out most of our money. Second, understand that most companies are motivated to settle with you on a balance you owe if you are already delinquent—meaning you haven't paid them in a while. They will more than likely accept a fraction of what you owe because they'd rather any money than no money. They also want to get the debt off of their books. This is the case for most debt including mortgages and credit cards. This is just like someone owing you $10,000 and they haven't paid you anything for over five years. If they say they can pay you $4,000 if you'll forgive the rest of the debt, you are more likely to accept the money and cancel the rest of the debt because at least you have something. You were able to recoup some of your money and the other $6,000 you'd just chunk up as a loss.

This is the same concept as a short sale is in the mortgage industry. Regardless of the type of debt, the important thing is to get an agreement in writing that the creditor agrees to the amount and considers the debt paid in full. The next important thing is to never give them access to your checking account; they may wipe you out.

False Help

The following service sometimes promises more than it actually delivers. Some say it appears to help the situation but only delays the inevitable or masks the root of the problem. False help is no help at all. One way people experience false help is through getting more debt, what they believe is temporary debt until they get back on their feet. One of the worst of these is payday loans. In most instances, you can't borrow your way out of debt. That is like asking an obese person to eat more junk food to get their body in better shape. You can't ask a person to eat their way out of obesity with the very food that got them there no more than you can borrow your way out of debt. (For those of you who are getting your pen, paper, and stamp together, my disclaimer… This is for a person who is obese because of poor eating habits, I am aware that there are various health reasons why people can become obese.)

Payday loans, if not paid back correctly, can result in catastrophic interest rates and fees. Payday loan establishments have also been accused of historically targeting the poor. They capitalize on people's bad habits and bank on the fact that if you're coming to them because you already don't have enough money, you'll continue the trend and end up in their quicksand of revolving fees and interest rates that make it virtually impossible to get out.

If you lend money to my people, to any of the down-and-out among you, don't come down hard on them and gouge them with interest. Exodus 22:25 The Message

Real Help

If you feel you need outside help you should consider counseling. Counseling is considered to be true help because it is based on teaching the individual about money. You get the advantage of another set of eyes, a person who is not in your condition, but can see your situation. They are not close enough to have an ulterior motive and are far enough to see your situation for what it is. Sometimes when we are trapped in a situation, we're too involved to see the exit doors. Picture a mouse in a maze trying to find the cheese but doesn't know which path to take, the scientist conducting the experiment can stand above the entire maze and see the necessary turns the mouse needs to take to get out of the maze. We're the mouse and the counselor is the scientist. Let them guide you out of your financial maze. Counseling help is provided through various churches and non-profit organizations, books, radio and T.V. shows, and I hope you would say this book offered you true help as well. Even though the books and T.V. shows aren't talking about your exact situation, you can gain wisdom from reading and observing principles and other people's state of affairs and then apply them to your individual situation.

Foolish for Fico

I talked about credit repair earlier and one indication the financial industry uses to determine if you have good or bad credit is your FICO score. Your credit score is called a FICO score and is a formula-based number that signifies your credit worthiness. FICO stands for Fair Isaac Corporation and FICO is its symbol on the New York Stock Exchange. Companies use your FICO score to determine the interest rates they offer you on such purchases as homes, cars, and credit cards. Your credit score is based on your credit history and is made up of five different segments: Payment History, Amounts Owed, Length of Credit History, New Credit, and Types of Credit Used. In order to even have a credit score you must use credit. That's why you hear people say you need to establish credit. This means you need to go borrow money and pay it back on time so you can establish a credit score. One requirement to keep and maintain a high score, is you must continue to borrow money. This is the system that the financial industry uses and it is warned against in the Bible in Proverbs Chapter 22 Verse 7 where the warning is issued that the borrower is servant to the lender. Establishing credit, i.e. a credit score is all about you borrowing and establishing a life of servitude just to maintain a FICO score. When you decide to end your life of servanthood, that is to say stop borrowing money, your FICO score will go down and eventually you'll have no score at all. Here are examples of good life choices that may have bad FICO score implications:

- Closing credit cards, especially ones with a long history.
- Closing credit cards with a zero balance-This can lower your score because it lowers your debt-to-available-credit ratio-If you have a $0 balance on a credit card that has a $10,000 limit and close it, your available credit has now decreased by $10,000, which could lower your credit score.
- Stop borrowing money-A portion of your credit score depends on you actually having credit, ie) borrowing money. So if you stop borrowing money altogether, your score will decrease.

While you may make the decision to stop borrowing money to better your life, by industry standards, you are damaging your credit, but you can have a productive life without relying on a credit score. Buying a house is one big purchase that relies on a credit score but if you are planning on buying a house, the mortgage company can disregard your FICO score and do manual underwriting to figure your interest rate (if you are financing it). Hopefully one day the industry will understand how flawed the FICO scoring system is but until then this is what we're measured by. So what do you do? Trust God. You're depending on Him anyway, not a man-made number system. Keep your focus on His Word, walking by FAITH, not your FICO. Stick to your goals of getting out of debt, reducing or eliminating credit cards and paying off accounts and let the FICO chips fall where they may.

The Easy Way

Well some perceive it as easy. I'm talking about bankruptcy. I know there are many legitimate reasons why some people file for bankruptcy. Some may have a severe health problem that has caused them to reach their health insurance's maximum payout and they can't afford to pay their medical bills, etc. Circumstances like this are understandable. What I'm talking about are the frivolous, lazy and irresponsible reasons why people file for bankruptcy. Some people take no responsibility for their decisions and look for every loophole and excuse not to right their wrongs and they use bankruptcy as a scapegoat, an easy way out of accepting responsibility for your financial actions. If you are one who thinks you are getting over by declaring bankruptcy and not paying people back, including businesses you owe money to, please medicate on this scripture:

> *The wicked borrows and does not repay, but the righteous shows mercy and gives.* Psalms 37:21 NKJV

Things to Remember

- 3-day Rule
- Juggling Clown
- Eating away Obesity

- Quicksand
- Mouse in Maze
- False Help vs Real Help
- FICO

More Borrowing Scriptures

A prudent man sees danger and takes refuge, but the simple keep going and suffer for it. Proverbs 22:3 NIV

Owe no man any thing, but to love one another: for he that loveth another hath fulfilled the law. Romans 13:8 KJV

Don't guarantee to pay someone else's debt. If you don't have the money, you might lose your bed. Proverbs 22:27 CEV

Don't gamble on the pot of gold at the end of the rainbow, hocking your house against a lucky chance. The time will come when you have to pay up; you'll be left with nothing but the shirt on your back. Proverbs 22:26-27 The Message

Give to everyone what you owe them: If you owe taxes, pay taxes; if revenue, then revenue; if respect, then respect; if honor, then honor. Romans 13:7 NIV

Keep your lives free from the love of money and be content with what you have, because God has said, "Never will I leave you; never will I forsake you." Heb 13:5 NIV

They promise them freedom, while they themselves are slaves of depravity--for a man is a slave to whatever has mastered him. 2 Pet 2:19 NIV

Appendix

Money Resources

FREE Credit Reports

Make sure you take advantage of a free credit report every year. Once a year everyone in America can get a free credit report from each of the three credit bureaus—Equifax, Experian, and TransUnion. You can request one and your spouse can request one also. (If you have a spouse like I do, who doesn't want to be bothered with that type of stuff, just request one for them but get their permission first.) Just log unto www.annualcreditreport.com and get it immediately or you can call 1-877-322-8228 and receive within 15 days.

The site and the number are supported by the three credit bureaus. If you call the credit bureaus directly, you will hear a recording that reverts you back to the above number, so save yourself some time and just call the number. When you call you can speak or enter the responses with a touch-tone phone so make sure you have quiet surroundings if you plan on using voice. You can request reports from one, two, or all three companies on one phone call, but you enter the info one at a time. This is the info you'll need to know: name, date of birth (including year), social security number, and address. Call from your home phone because the site will recognize it and already have the address and name downloaded so you just verify it which will also save you time. For me, the site has my husband's name downloaded not mine, so when they ask if the name is correct, you can say no and then state your name. It takes 15 days to receive the paper reports. You can also request the reports in writing but why spend postage and unnecessary time. It's important to check your report every year to make sure it's accurate and to make sure no one has stolen your identity and opened up accounts in your name. **To get a free report every four months just space out your requests to a different credit bureau every four months and rotate the requests. Ex) Get one from Equifax in January, Experian in April, and Trans Union in August, then repeat the cycle each year.

Media Resources on Money

Websites

General

- www.PurseString.com
- www.crown.org
- www.practicalmoneyskills.com

Savings

- www.FeedThePig.org
- www.Choosetosave.org

Investing

- www.greekshares.com
- www.finweb.com/finlplan/savinves
- www.fool.com

Banking

- www.bankrate.com
- www.cardrate.com (to find a lower credit card % so you can pay the balance off faster)
- www.annualcreditreport.com

School

- www.Collegesavings.org
- www.Finaid.org
- www.Studentloans.gov
- www.Collegeboard.com
- www.Schwab.com/college

Credit Counseling

- www.TakeChargeAmerica.org (non-profit, offers free credit counseling)
- www.crown.org

Govt Resources

- www.Sec.gov/investor/oiea_podcasts.htm
- www.ncua.gov
- www.Usda.gov/personalfinance

Budgets

- www.Mymoney.gov
- www.mint.com.
- www.crown.org-free help-call Crown Financial Ministries at 1-800-722-1976

Mortgages
- http://www.ehow.com/facts_5817087_equity-line-vs_-reverse-mortgage.html
- http://reversemortgageguides.org
- www.mint.com
  www.ftc.gov/bcp/edu/pubs/consumer/homes/rea13.shtm

Teaching Moments for Children/Internet Games

- www.federalreserveeducation.org
- www.Lemonadestand.org
- www.Coolmath.com (coffee shop and lemonade stand game for kids)
- www.themint.org
- www.practicalmoneyskills.com/games

    Cash Puzzler
    Countdown to Retirement
    Ed's Bank
    Financial Football
    Financial Soccer
    Money Metropolis
    Peter Pig's Money Counter
    Road Trip to Savings
    Smart Money Quiz Show

- www.apples4theteacher.com/math.html
- www.orangekids.com (1st to 6th grade)
- www.richkidsmartkid.com (K to 12th grade)
- www.mysavingsquest.com
- www.mykidsbank.org
- www.usmint.gov/kids/
- http://senseanddollars.thinkport.org (Teens)

- http://bizkids.com/ (Preteens)
- www.italladdsup.org (HighSchool)
- www.mathwire.com/money/money/html

Radio Shows

- Dave Ramsey Show or www.daveramsey.com
- Crown Financial Ministries or www.crown.org
- The Clark Howard Show or www.clarkhoward.com

T.V. Shows

- The Suze Orman Show
- Til Debt Do Us Part (Gail Vaz-Oxlade)
- Your Life, Your Money (www.pbs.org/your-life-your-money/)
- Families Stand Together (www.pbs.org/parents/familiesstandtogether/)

Videos/DVDs

- Maxed Out
- The Great Misunderstanding by Dave Ramsey

Board Games

- Rich Dad Cashflow
- Life
- Monopoly
- Wits and Wagers
- Pay Day

Suggested Reading

If you want more in depth information, below is a list of books that I personally recommend that correspond to each chapter in this book. The Holy Bible, my absolute favorite, of course covers not only all of the chapters, but is the first source for all aspects of life. Any book pales in comparison to the Holy Bible and is not even worthy of being mentioned in the same sentence.

Faith

- *The Case for a Creator* by Lee Stroebel
- *The Case for Christ* by Lee Stroebel
- *The Purpose-Driven Life* by Rick Warren
- *It's Your Time* by Joel Osteen

Obedience

- *Idea Tithing* by Mark Victor Hansen
- *The Miracle of Tithing* by Mark Victor Hansen

Giving

- *Boundaries* by Henry Cloud & Dr. John Townsend
- *Approval Addiction* by Joyce Meyer

Living your Dreams

- *48 Days To the Work You Love* by Dan Miller
- *Reposition Yourself: Living Life Without Limits* by T.D.Jakes
- *The One Minute Entrepreneur* by Ken Blanchard
- *EntreLeadership* by Dave Ramsey

Planning

- *The Total Money Makeover* by Dave Ramsey
- *The Millionaire Zone* by Jennifer Openshaw
- *The Success Principles* by Jack Canfield with Janet Switzer
- *The Money Class* by Suze Orman

Saving

- *The Millionaire Next Door* by Dr. Thomas J. Stanley & Dr. William D. Danko
- *Start Late, Finish Rich* by David Bach
- *Stop Acting Rich* by Dr. Thomas J. Stanley
- *Living Large in Lean Times* by Clark Howard

Borrowing

- *More Than Enough* by Dave Ramsey
- *Young, Fabulous & Broke* by Suze Orman
- *Debt-proof Your Marriage* by Mary Hunt
- *Debt Free for Life* by David Bach

Bibliography

"God, Money & Your Faith." *www.crown.org*. Crown Financial Ministries. http://www.crown.org/Library/ViewArticle.aspx?ArticleId=803.

Dictionary.com LLC. *www.dictionary.com*. Definitions of superstitions, asset, savings, liability, envy, pride, jealousy, and coveting. May 23, 2012. October 25, 2012.

Bergman, Andrew, Grusin Dave. "Good Times" theme song. *www.lyricsondemand.com*. http://www.lyricsondemand.com/tvthemes/goodtimeslyrics.html.

Loomis J. Carol. "The $600 Billion Challenge." *Fortune Magazine*, July 5, 2010 p82 and *Fortune* on *www.CNN Money.com* http://features.blogs.fortune.cnn.com/2010/06/16/gates-buffett-600-billion-dollar-philanthropy-challenge/.

Bach, David. *Start Late, Finish Rich*. New York: Broadway Books, 2005.

Ehrenreich, Barbara. *Nickel and Dimed: On (Not) Getting By in America*. New York: Metropolitan Books, 2001.

GIVE THE GIFT OF *A Christian's Worst Witne$$* TO YOUR FRIENDS AND COLLEAGUES

☐ **YES,** I want _____ copies of *A Christian's Worst Witne$$* for $14.95 each, and _____ copies of the companion workbook for $9.95ea.

☐ **YES,** I am interested in having Shalonda McFarland speak or give a seminar to my church, company, association, school, or organization. Please send me information.

Include $3.00 shipping and handling for one book, and $2.00 for each additional book.

Payment must accompany orders. Allow 7 days for delivery.

My check or money order for $ _____ is enclosed. Please charge my ☐ **Visa** ☐ **MasterCard** ☐ **American Express**

Name_____

Organization_____

Address_____

City/State/Zip_____

Phone_____Email_____

Card # _____

Exp. Date _____**Signature**_____

☐ **Email orders**: Info@ShalondaMcfarland.com
☐ **Fax orders:** (281) 446-6709 Fax this form.
☐ **Postal orders: Shalonda McFarland,**
    P.O. Box 62425,
    Houston, TX 77205, USA.
☐ **Internet orders: www.shalondamcfarland.com**

GIVE THE GIFT OF *A Christian's Worst Witne$$*
TO YOUR FRIENDS AND COLLEAGUES

☐ **YES**, I want ____ copies of *A Christian's Worst Witne$$* for $14.95 each, and ____ copies of the companion workbook for $9.95ea.

☐ **YES**, I am interested in having Shalonda McFarland speak or give a seminar to my church, company, association, school, or organization. Please send me information.

Include $3.00 shipping and handling for one book, and $2.00 for each additional book.

Payment must accompany orders. Allow 7 days for delivery.

My check or money order for $ _____ is enclosed. Please charge my ☐ **Visa** ☐ **MasterCard** ☐ **American Express**

Name_____

Organization _____

Address_____

City/State/Zip_____

Phone_____ Email_____

Card # _____

Exp. Date _____ **Signature**_____

- **Email orders**: Info@ShalondaMcfarland.com
- **Fax orders:** (281) 446-6709 Fax this form.
- **Postal orders:** Shalonda McFarland,
  P.O. Box 62425,
  Houston, TX 77205, USA.
- **Internet orders:** www.shalondamcfarland.com

www.ingramcontent.com/pod-product-compliance
Lightning Source LLC
Chambersburg PA
CBHW050634300426
44112CB00012B/1797